HOW TO STEAL AN ELECTION

ALSO BY DAVID MOORE

The Superpollsters

HOW TO STEAL AN
ELECTION

THE INSIDE STORY OF
HOW GEORGE BUSH'S BROTHER AND FOX NETWORK
MISCALLED
THE 2000 ELECTION AND
CHANGED THE COURSE OF HISTORY

DAVID W. MOORE

NATION BOOKS
www.nationbooks.org
New York

HOW TO STEAL AN ELECTION

Published by
Nation Books
An Imprint of Avalon Publishing Group, Inc.
245 West 17th Street, 11th Floor
New York, NY 10011

AVALON
publishing group incorporated

Nation Books is a co-publishing venture of the Nation Institute and Avalon
Publishing Group Incorporated.

Library of Congress Cataloging-in-Publication Data

ISBN-10: 1-56025-929-9
ISBN-13: 978-1-56025-929-9

9 8 7 6 5 4 3 2 1

Book design by Pauline Neuwirth, Neuwirth & Associates, Inc.

Printed in the United States of America
Distributed by Publishers Group West

To Zelda

Contents

Acknowledgments

My sincere appreciation to all the people who agreed to be interviewed for this book. I am especially grateful to Warren Mitofsky, who gave me the opportunity to observe the CBS/CNN decision team on Election Night 2000, and who has been unfailingly patient over the past several years in answering all my questions about the election night projection system and related matters. He and his partner, Joe Lenski, who has also put up with my many questions with the utmost patience, have both been invaluable resources for this book. I am also very grateful to Cynthia Talkov, who spent many hours with me going over the events of Election Night 2000. Murray Edelman also spent considerable time with me, reviewing the details of Election Night 2000 and the operations of the Voter News Service. John Blydenburgh gave me a different and important perspective on the election night projection system, including what happened in 2000 as well as earlier events in 1994. Other people who provided important information include Kathleen Frankovic, Sheldon Gawiser, David Pace, Dan Merkle, Clyde Tucker, Trevor Tompson, Inga Parsons, Mark Schulman and Mike Curtin.

Thanks to Martha Barron Barrett, for her helpful insights in the early stages of the project; Reid Boates, my agent, for his work with the book, but also his sage advice and enthusiasm for the project; and John Oakes and Carl Bromley of Nation Books, co-publisher and editor, respectively, whose suggestions have greatly improved the book.

For their abiding support for my writing efforts, special thanks to Allison, Eric, Josh, and Leeyanne. And to Zelda...xybmbtmb mzbyzcxu.

Preface

The presidential election of 2000 was stolen from Al Gore. This is an historical observation, not a partisan charge. The observation is no more partisan than acknowledging that supporters of Lyndon Baines Johnson helped steal the 1948 Democratic senatorial primary in Texas from Coke Stevenson, allowing LBJ to be elected U.S. senator—and change the course of history. There have been many other cases of stolen elections in American history, of course, though typically evidence of such thefts takes decades to emerge.[1] In the present case, investigations in the past six years have revealed a series of events that provide evidence of theft beyond a reasonable doubt.

Let me clarify what I mean by saying election 2000 was stolen. Al Gore won the national popular vote for president of the United States by about half a million votes, though officially he lost the election because he did not receive a majority of the electoral votes. Had he been declared the winner in Florida, he would have won both the electoral and popular vote. Officially, Gore lost Florida to George W. Bush by 537 votes. In fact, the evidence shows that more people in Florida voted for Gore than for Bush by a margin of at least several thousand votes. Many of those votes were not counted because of ballot designs, especially in Palm Beach (the infamous "butterfly" ballot) and Duval counties, but these uncounted votes do not constitute theft by themselves. Some of these votes were left uncounted not because of partisan mischief, but because of genuine mistakes for which the law provides no clear remedy. But there were other uncounted votes that could have been counted for which the law did provide a remedy, but which the U.S. Supreme Court denied.

The theft of the Florida election, and thus the presidency, resulted from illegal actions taken before the election by high Florida officials, including Governor Jeb Bush and Secretary of State Katherine Harris, to deprive qualified Florida citizens from exercising their right to vote—costing Gore tens of thousands of votes. The theft also resulted from the illegally partisan actions of Florida and other officials after the election to prevent a fair hand recount in the state, as provided by law, and to count probable ballots for Bush that had been cast after Election Day. The theft was ultimately assured when the U.S. Supreme Court decided to halt the Florida recount and essentially award the presidency to Bush, a decision that is widely seen among legal experts as unprincipled and without legal justification.

In the midst of all the illegal activities both before and after the election was the networks' erroneous projection of Bush as the next president of the United States at about a quarter past two in the morning Eastern Time on election night. There was nothing illegal or unethical about that projection—it was just an unusual error, apparently caused by faulty data. Yet, in one of those rare twists of fate, it's quite possible that had the mistake not been made, the efforts to steal the election would not have succeeded. The projection led to Gore's conceding the election to Bush, then retracting the concession a couple of hours later as the vote count revealed the election to be a toss-up. But the damage had been done. For the next thirty-six days after the election, the conservative media continually lambasted Gore for being a sore loser and trying to "steal" the election, while even the mainstream media treated the attempts at recount as though it were a bizarre circus rather than a serious attempt to determine what Florida voters really intended. Had the networks not made the projection and given the illusion that Bush had won, a very different political environment would have greeted the two candidates after the election, one that would have been more propitious for Gore's efforts to obtain a statewide hand recount of all the votes—and quite likely victory.

Regardless of whether Gore would have prevailed even with the improved environment, the networks' miscall by itself is worth examining. It turns out that the projection of Bush as the Florida winner at 2:16 in the morning Eastern Time was caused not so much by erroneous data, as all the networks claimed after the election, but by the respective networks' decision teams making poor judgments—succumbing to competitive pressures to beat the other networks to make the call, or at least not to be last, though the data demanded caution. Most ironically of all, the whole series of network calls was triggered not by statistical analyses showing Bush would emerge the winner, but by Bush's brother urging his cousin at Fox network to make the call—even as Bush's lead in the statewide vote count was rapidly declining.

It is a fascinating story, not only what happened with the networks on election night, but the context within which the erroneous projection turned out to have such a profound impact on the political environment, and ultimately on the history of the world. For there can be little doubt that the Bush presidency has given the United States, and indeed the whole world, a very different history from what would have been had Gore become president. The networks apologized for interfering in the democratic process, but they blamed their media consortium for providing faulty data, when the consortium itself warned against using the data to make the projection. Now, with a new consortium and a few technical adjustments, the networks would have us believe that the problems of the past have been solved. But the networks have done little to constrain the competitive environment, and future mistakes are inevitable.

It's unlikely that a miscall in the future will have as much of an impact on the electoral process as the erroneous projection for Bush in 2000. Still, we can't be sure. No one would have predicted the sequence of events that led to George W. Bush's very improbable assumption of the presidency and the theft of the election from Al Gore. But it happened.

In my heart, I do believe that democracy was harmed
by my network and others on November 7, 2000.

—*Roger Ailes, chairman and CEO of
Fox News Network, February 14, 2001*

1

Irreparable Harm
An Overview

"Jebbie says we got it! Jebbie says we got it!"

Those were the words uttered by John Ellis about a quarter after two in the morning following Election Night 2000, moments before the Fox network projected George W. Bush the winner over Al Gore in Florida, and thus the next president of the United States. This was not the first projection Fox and the other networks had made for the Sunshine State. Shortly before eight the previous evening, when Florida's pivotal role in the election was still not evident, the networks had projected Al Gore to win, though the call was rescinded about two hours later. But by two in the morning, everyone knew that if Bush won Florida, he won the presidency.

The man who uttered the crucial words that led to Fox's projection of Bush as the winner in Florida was the head of Fox's decision team, responsible for projecting the winners in all the statewide contests on election night. John Ellis is also the cousin of George W. and Jeb Bush, at that time the governors of Texas and Florida, respectively. (Ellis's mother, Nancy Ellis, is the sister of former President George H. W. Bush.) For much of the previous evening and early morning, Ellis had been on the phone with his cousins, who were both at the same location in Austin, Texas. "It was just the three of us guys handing the phone back and forth," he told *The New Yorker*, the following week, "me with the numbers, one of them a governor, the other the President-elect. Now, that was cool."[1]

The catalyst for projecting his cousin as the winner in Florida, Ellis wrote in the December 11 and 26 2000, issues of *Inside* magazine,[2] was his calculation of a "need/get" ratio — the percentage of the outstanding vote that Gore needed to catch up to Bush versus the percentage of the vote that Gore would actually get. At five minutes before two, Ellis wrote, "it became clear to me that Gore could not win. I called George W. and asked him what he thought." Bush turned the question around and asked Ellis what he thought. "I think you've got it," Ellis said. After discussing the need/get ratio with George W. for a little while, they signed off. A few minutes later, according to Ellis, after the need/get ratio showed that the gap between what Gore needed and what he would get was eight percentage points, "we called Florida for Bush."

That account is substantially different from what actually happened, according to the statistician who sat next to Ellis all during the afternoon, evening, and next morning of Fox's 2000 presidential election coverage. Cynthia Talkov was, according to Ellis, his "statistical wizard," the one person on the Fox decision team who "knew the [voter projection] system inside out, knew the details and pitfalls of each and every estimator on our screens." But she never saw Ellis making any calculations for a need/get ratio, nor was there such a ratio displayed on the screens.[3] There were several different screens that could have been used to make such an estimate, but she did not see Ellis perusing the screens and making the calculations. Instead he was chatting with one or the other of his cousins on the phone. Suddenly he stood up and announced, "Jebbie says we got it! Jebbie says we got it!" Almost immediately, the decision team projected Bush the winner, with the announcement made on the Fox network moments later. For all practical purposes, Jeb Bush had just called the election for his brother.

The official records show that Fox made that announcement at 2:16 in the morning. Within four minutes, NBC, CBS, CNN, and ABC followed suit, all now proclaiming Bush as the next president of the United States. Lying on the floor in his campaign's staff room, on the seventh floor of the Loew's Hotel in Nashville, his chin propped up in his hands, Gore absorbed the news with his staff members in shocked silence. Moments later, lumbering to his feet, he said, "I want to concede. I want to be gracious about this."[4] Ten minutes later, he called Bush to offer his concession and good wishes, and then he and his entourage set out for Nashville's War Memorial Plaza, where he would make the concession public.

As it turned out, of course, the projection by all the networks was wrong. When they made the call, Bush had not won in Florida. In fact, it would take more than a month before Bush was finally declared the winner, though a post-election analysis of the Florida votes shows that more people in that state voted for Gore than Bush. After reviewing the results of that study, conducted by the National Opinion Research Center at the University of Chicago,[5] CBS News and the Associated Press both concluded, "Under any standard that tabulated all disputed votes statewide, Gore erased Bush's advantage and emerged with a tiny lead that ranged from 42 to 171 votes."[6] *The Washington Post* echoed that conclusion: "The efforts of a consortium of news organizations to revisit the election controversy yielded a simple, even sensational, revelation: If there had been some way last fall to recount every vote—undervotes and overvotes alike, in all 67 Florida counties—former vice president Al Gore likely would be in the White House." The author went on to write, "The results plainly suggest that more Floridians intended to cast votes for him [Gore] than Bush, and that under most standards for counting ballots by hand he would have won in a statewide recount."[7]

Within two hours after declaring Bush the winner, the networks had all retracted their projections. In the meantime, as Bush's lead dwindled, Gore changed his mind about a public concession, and called an irritated George Bush to give him the news. When the Texas governor responded by saying that his "little brother" had assured him he had won the state, Gore said, "Let me explain something. Your little brother is not the ultimate authority on this."[8] Little did Gore realize at the time how influential the "little brother" Jeb Bush had been in the networks' erroneous projections, and thus Gore's near-public concession.

It is difficult to overestimate the impact of the erroneous network call on the post-election political environment. It created havoc for Gore, giving rise to charges that he was a "sore loser" and undermining the legitimacy of his efforts to obtain a hand recount of the votes in Florida. Even some conservatives acknowledged the problem. Reed Irvine and Cliff Kincaid of Accuracy in Media noted, "The result of this [network projection for Bush] was that the Bush campaign and his supporters believed that they had won, and it was now being stolen away."[9] That clearly was the view of Fox's conservative commentator, Sean Hannity, who asserted repeatedly during the network's post-election coverage, "The vice president because of his blind ambition has brought us to the brink of a constitutional crisis." Hannity also charged the Democrats who were pressing for a vote recount in Florida with trying "to steal the election."[10]

Irvine and Kincaid went on to cite Steve Luxenberg of *The Washington Post*, who wrote, "The networks' call had a huge psychological effect on the electorate and the candidates, with political and historical ramifications. Voters might have shrugged off a long count in Florida as an acceptable delay in a contested election. But a 'reversal' fed the notion of a tainted result, contributed to the overheated rhetoric on both sides . . . and helped fuel the sense of a country in crisis."[11] The perception of a "reversal"—that Bush was the winner, but now Gore was trying to overturn the results—was caused by the erroneous network projection that left millions of people going to bed on election night believing that the Texas governor was the next president, and millions of other people waking up the next morning to read their newspapers with the same misinformation. Among other newspapers with such headlines were the *Boston Globe, USA Today, New York Post, San Francisco Chronicle, Philadelphia Inquirer, Washington Times, Sacramento Bee, St. Louis Post-Dispatch, Austin (Texas) American-Statesman*— along with at least three Florida newspapers, the *Miami Herald, Orlando Sentinel,* and *Tallahassee Democrat*.[12]

The miscall and the hostile environment for Gore that it created no doubt also affected the vice president's recount strategy in Florida and perhaps even ultimately the Supreme Court decision that effectively handed the election to Bush. Among Gore's advisors, a major concern was to avoid reinforcing the perception of Gore as a sore loser,[13] an image the Republicans were actively trying to foster. Many in the news media treated Gore's efforts to get a hand recount as a losing battle that should not be fought. As Todd Gitlin wrote in the *Los Angeles Times,* even NBC's Tim Russert, a Democrat who had worked at different times for New York Senator Patrick Moynihan and New York Governor Mario Cuomo, was "telling viewers no fewer than three times on Nov. 8 [the day after the election] that the way things were going in Florida . . . it was time for Al Gore to play statesman and concede." Gitlin added, "Not one barking head ever suggested that Bush concede under any conditions whatever."[14]

A logical strategy urged on Gore by some of his advisors was to ask for a recount in each of the sixty-seven Florida counties. He eventually proposed this idea to Bush, but did not initiate action immediately on his own. When Bush got the proposal, he dismissed it out of hand. Had there been a full statewide hand recount, the media consortium recount showed, Gore almost surely would have won. Instead, his team tried to identify the counties where Gore might be able to pick up enough votes quickly to justify his fight in Florida, all the while fighting the image of his being an obstructionist to the will of the people. But the media consortium also showed that if a limited hand recount had been authorized as Gore's legal team initially requested, it was still quite possible that Bush would have emerged the victor. Only if there were hand recounts in all the counties would a Gore win have been almost certain. And that did not happen.

But it almost did. Despite Gore's limited recount request, District Court Judge Terry Lewis was apparently set to order a full hand recount across the state of both the undervotes and overvotes, when the Supreme Court ordered all counties in Florida to stop whatever recount efforts were under way.[15] As Florida Representative Peter Deustch said at the congressional hearing, "The Supreme Court's political decision of stopping the counting of the votes was in fact influenced by the missed [network] calls of calling Bush the President. If there was no winner after November 7, I think the political decision very well might have been different."[16]

The logic behind such an assertion comes from the justification for the recount halt, authored by Justice Antonin Scalia, which essentially assumed that Bush was the real winner in Florida. Scalia wrote that to continue the counting would "threaten irreparable harm to the petitioner [Bush] and to the country, by casting a cloud upon what he claims to be the legality of his election."[17] That is an amazing assertion, for it clearly assumes what the vote count had not definitively demonstrated—that Bush had won more votes in Florida than Gore. Not to allow the recount would have been of "irreparable harm" to Gore, and also to the country, if one assumes that Gore might have emerged the winner. Only if one assumes that Bush was the real winner would Scalia's justification be defensible. But on what grounds could Scalia and the other four justices assume that Bush was the real winner? It would appear that the networks' miscall, and the resulting political environment in Florida and Washington, D.C., which treated Gore's fight for a vote recount as doomed and destructive, helped shape, if not determine, the Supreme Court's decision.

The argument against this theory is that the five justices who voted to give Bush the election would have done so regardless of what the networks did or the what the political environment happened to be. But Justice David Souter believed that he was very close to persuading

Justice Anthony Kennedy to send the case back to the Florida justices to fix whatever was necessary to have a fair count. Kennedy had initially joined with Justices William Rehnquist, Clarence Thomas, Antonin Scalia, and Sandra Day O'Connor to temporarily halt the recount, but in the final decision he seemed to be wavering. Souter told a group of prep-school students a month after the Supreme Court decision that if he'd had "one more day—just one more day," he might have prevailed. But Kennedy thought that the prospect of more political fighting was too much for the country to endure.[18] It's also true that had the political environment been different, had the presidential contest been seen as the tie it was rather than as a fight by a sore loser who had conceded, and then un-conceded, and was now trying to hang on to power, Kennedy's objection to the continued political fighting would have been moot. With no presumed winner, the only fair way to determine who won would be to let the votes decide. Only if Kennedy assumed that the winner had already been identified could he justify his argument against continuing the recount.

MANY COMMENTATORS EXPRESSED astonishment that Fox would hire a person so closely related to one of the two principal candidates to head its decision desk. This was an obvious conflict of interest, which Fox never acknowledged but instead defended as non-discrimination against relatives of politicians. The person who invented exit polls in the 1960s and developed the election night projection system the networks were using that night is Warren Mitofsky, who characterized Ellis's actions—conferring with his cousins while heading the Fox decision desk—as "the most unprofessional election night work I could ever imagine. He had no business talking to the Bush brothers or to any other politician about what he was doing."[19]

One might have expected Fox and Ellis to take a serious hit in the journalistic and polling community because of Ellis's behavior that evening, but that didn't happen. They were let off the hook, ironically, by Mitofsky himself, who on Election Night 2000 was the co director of the joint CBS/CNN decision desk. He told Seth Mnookin of *Brill's Content*, "this business about Fox pressuring other people to call, I never made a projection in my life because of some other network. When I heard they put it [the projection for Bush] out there, I was disappointed, because I wanted to do it . . . we were about to make the projection."[20]

From that comment and other reviews of the data provided by VNS on election night, it soon became the accepted wisdom that if Fox had not made the call at the time it did, the other networks would have done so not much later. Slate's Jack Shafer wrote a week after the election: "It's somewhat hilarious that the press ethicists are calling for the head of John Ellis, the Fox News prognosticator and Bush cousin who gave Florida to Bush contemporaneously with the networks. Although Ellis has been fairly upfront about rooting for his cousin, we need to remember that he was looking at the same data as Mitofsky and the other network seers who made the same call."[21]

But a closer investigation into how the networks made the calls suggests that, contrary to conventional wisdom, had Fox not made the call, the other networks would have also refrained. NBC was the second network to make the call, but at the time of Fox's announcement, the NBC decision team leader, Sheldon Gawiser, was on the phone with Murray Edelman, the editorial director of VNS. Edelman was explaining why it would not be a good idea to call Bush the winner, but when Fox's announcement hit the air, Gawiser cut the connection to call the election for Bush. At that moment, I was sitting next to Mitofsky and Lenski, who were reviewing the computer screens, to see whether they wanted to follow Fox. When NBC made its call, Mitofsky immediately announced that CNN and CBS would do so as well. Despite the other networks' projections, the ABC decision desk was against making a projection, but an ABC executive overrode that decision and called Bush the winner in Florida, just four minutes after Fox. The Associated Press and VNS refrained from hopping on the Fox bandwagon. Two hours later, they were vindicated when all the networks rescinded their projections.

This book presents a detailed account of the crucial decisions made by each network that led to the fiasco on Election Night 2000. It shows how the Fox decision team was led astray by the constant communication between Ellis and the Bush brothers, and how the Fox projection triggered similar decisions by the other networks—though the original call should never have been made. The book also shows why it was possible for NBC's Gawiser, and the CBS/CNN team of Mitofsky and Lenski, to succumb to competitive pressure once Fox had called the election, but why they almost certainly would have resisted sticking their necks out had Fox not made the call first.

Although the networks all agreed that their actions on Election Night 2000 harmed the electoral process, they have done little to prevent similar blunders in the future. They blamed VNS for the problems on Election Night 2000, essentially excusing their decision teams for making hasty decisions and avoiding the real issue of network competition. Yet, it was competition more than any other factors that gave rise to the most serious blunder—the projection of Bush as the winner in Florida, which created havoc in the post-election fight for the presidency. By 2004, the networks had disbanded VNS and signed on with a new election night projection system, headed by Mitofsky and Lenski. But the networks refused to close down their individual decision teams. They continue to compete with each other and risk making miscalls in the process. In 2004, the decision teams were cautious, with Election 2000 still fresh in their minds. But as Mitofsky warns: "In my opinion, nothing can keep the networks from someday calling another race incorrectly."[22]

On Election Day 2000, television news organizations staged
a collective drag race on the crowded highway of democracy,
recklessly endangering the electoral process, the political life
of the country, and their own credibility, all for reasons that
may be conceptually flawed and commercially questionable.

—Television's Performance on Election Night 2000:
A Report for CNN, *January 29, 2001*

2

Election Night Projections
A Brief History

In the summer of 1967, CBS hired a quiet-spoken, dark-haired, full-bearded, thirty-two-year-old statistician from the U.S. Census Bureau to run the network's election night operation. Over the next four decades, Warren Mitofsky would revolutionize the way networks called the election, invent exit polls, design a vote-projection system that is still being used today, head the first network consortium election night projection system, leave the consortium under less-than-ideal circumstances to found his own exit poll company, become an election night consultant for CNN and CBS who needed him to compete against the other networks, and—after the Election Night 2000 disaster, followed by the meltdown of the exit poll operation on Election Night 2002— stage a Charles de Gaulle–like return once again to head (along with his younger colleague, Joe Lenski) the new network consortium. In the process, with his blunt, no-nonsense style and his disinclination to suffer fools gladly, Mitofsky would become the dominant personality in his field, angering some people in the industry, earning respect from most. Today, with a distinctive gravely voice, the white-haired, clean-shaven dean of exit polls often appears on national television programs to explain the intricacies and, more recently, the problems of election night polling.

WHEN MITOFSKY WAS hired by CBS in 1967, his principal mission was to devise a sound, statistical method for accurately and quickly projecting winners on election night. For the three previous elections, 1962 to 1966, the network had employed pollster Louis Harris, who developed the first election night projection system for television.[1] His "Vote Profile Analysis" system consisted of identifying eighty key precincts in each state, with the precincts constituting a more or less representative sample of voting districts across that state. Many of the precincts were "tag" precincts, which meant they were "tagged" as homogeneous with respect to some major characteristic— mostly Catholic or Protestant, white collar, blue collar, urban, rural, black, or white. Data were fed into an IBM computer to project the winner in each race.

Initially, this system worked beautifully. In 1962, it allowed CBS to beat NBC (ABC emerged as a competitor later) in projecting winners in thirteen senatorial and gubernatorial races in seven states. Harris's system also allowed CBS to report how the vote broke down by types of voters. Until then, the networks could only report the raw numbers— who was ahead and by how much, but nothing about how the vote compared by types of voters. Now, using Harris's "tag" precincts, CBS could provide greater insight, comparing results between blacks and whites, Catholics and Protestants, and the poor and the rich.[2]

By 1966, the other two networks had caught up with CBS, and Harris's system showed its flaws. It produced incorrect CBS projections in the gubernatorial contests in both Maryland and Georgia. The pollsters had been selecting his sample precincts using quota sampling, rather than the more advanced scientific method of probability sampling, and CBS executives wanted Harris to adjust his models.

But he was reluctant to do so. That was his last election at CBS, though the network kept him on contract through 1968, to prevent him from working for the opposition. With Harris gone, the network was determined to hire a statistical expert to run its election night operation. That expert was Warren Mitofsky.

Virtually all of Mitofsky's activities at CBS for the first two years focused on developing a statistically based projection system. However useless such an enterprise might appear to outside observers, to CBS the competition to be the best at projecting winners on election night was sacrosanct. And the other networks were no less committed to this endeavor. Being first, they determined, meant money in the bank. But being right was essential.

There was a minor problem with the instructions that William Leonard, head of CBS News, gave to Mitofsky when he joined CBS. Accuracy and speed in projecting winners are inherently contradictory goals. The longer one waits for the votes to come in, the more likely the projection will be correct. The flip side, of course: Very early projections are more likely to be wrong. What should Mitofsky do, he asked Leonard after getting his instructions—"crap-shoot" the election, going all out for speed with the attendant risk of being wrong, or make later projections that would more likely be correct?

Leonard said he wanted both accuracy and speed.

"But suppose you had one hundred dollars," Mitofsky said, "and you had to divide it between speed and accuracy, how much would you spend on each?"

Leonard said, "I want a hundred dollars on speed. And a hundred dollars on accuracy."

Nothing more was said about the issue until the following year. The weekend before the election, Leonard came into Mitofsky's office. "I don't care how long it takes," he said. "I want to be right."

That was what Mitofsky wanted to hear. "I never heard another word about how quick our projections were until after the 1980 elections."[3]

★

ONE OF THE earliest innovations that Mitofsky introduced was exit polling. The idea for this operation came from a market researcher who interviewed moviegoers immediately after they had seen a motion picture. He wanted to get feedback that the movie company could use to revise a film before distributing it more widely. Mitofsky saw the utility of the method for his own research. It would be a good idea to interview voters immediately after they had cast their ballot, so he could get a good preliminary idea of how election night would turn out once the actual vote tabulations were reported.

His first opportunity to experiment with this idea came in the 1967 Kentucky gubernatorial race. He chose the sample precincts in the state on the basis of scientific sampling methods, so that the overall set of precincts would represent a statistically valid microcosm of the electorate as a whole. The interviewers assigned to each precinct would approach voters after they exited the polling booths, ask them if they would fill out a brief ballot, and then hand the respondents a brief paper ballot that could be deposited in a special CBS ballot box nearby. The interviewers would not approach all voters—just every third, or fifth, or tenth voter, depending on how many were needed in that precinct. Nor would the interviewers continue the effort throughout the day, but rather at specified discrete periods in the morning, mid-day, and afternoon. At the end of each period, they would call in the information to a central location, where it was immediately entered into a computer.

By the end of the day, even before the polls had closed, Mitofsky already had a pretty good idea of how the election would turn out. But he did not call the election on the basis of these exit poll results. Instead, he compared the actual vote count throughout the evening from his sample precincts with the exit poll results— and when they agreed, he felt comfortable in projecting the winner.

In 1968, CBS used exit polls in six state presidential primaries, as well as in twenty-one states during the general election. By 1970, Mitofsky had lengthened his ballot to include several demographic questions (like gender, income, age, and party), as well as attitude questions on salient issues. The exit polls thus became a useful analytic tool, far superior to the "tag precincts" invented by Harris, for analyzing the vote. It was not until 1973 that NBC first embraced exit polls for that purpose, and 1980 when ABC finally followed suit.

During Election Night 1980, NBC upped the competitive ante by calling the presidential contests in several states using only exit poll results. Until then, exit polls had been used only to help verify vote count and explain election results. As predictive tools, they are highly unreliable. One might think that because they include interviews of voters immediately after they have cast ballots, the poll results would be especially accurate. But it turns out that there are so many problems with the conduct of exit polls, they are often further off the mark than pre-election telephone polls, which are taken days before an election and include many people who say they will vote but don't. Such was dramatically demonstrated on Election Night 2004, when the national exit poll showed John Kerry winning the presidency over George W. Bush by three percentage points, while most of the pre-election telephone polls accurately showed Bush winning by a small margin.

For the 1980 presidential election, all three networks conducted national exit polls, with sample precincts spread throughout the country. In these national samples, there are not enough precincts in any given state to call the statewide contests, so NBC conducted additional exit polls in each of several states where the presidential race was expected to be competitive. The network was determined to reassert its leadership on election night, and call the presidential winner before the other two networks. Reagan's vote surge over the weekend immensely helped that goal. By 8:15 in the evening Eastern Time on Election Day, long before there was substantial vote count in most of the states, NBC had projected Reagan the winner in twenty-two states with 270 electoral votes—and the next president of the United States. Eleven of those states were projected solely on the basis of exit polls.

The other two networks were stunned. Although everyone knew by that time that Reagan would eventually win the election, especially once California added its electoral vote total later in the evening, neither CBS nor ABC had any legitimate way to make the projection. On election night, winning the presidency is not about winning the popular vote; it's about winning enough states to produce 270 electoral votes. That meant that the two networks had to wait until sufficient votes were reported in each state, so they could project a winner. The votes are not counted until the polls are closed, and at 8:15— when NBC made its projections—many polls were still open.

The truth is that even NBC should not have called the race that early. Mitofsky later claimed that in five of the twenty-two races, the vote was so close at the time NBC made the projection, either Carter or Reagan could have won those states. But to NBC it probably didn't matter, because even if it was wrong in one of the eastern states, once the results came in from the West the electoral vote total would eventually be in Reagan's favor. And, as Mitofsky acknowledged, even the five states that shouldn't have been called so early eventually went for Reagan.

Carter was scheduled to give a news conference at ten in the evening Eastern Time, when he would undoubtedly concede the election. According to Mitofsky, "ABC raced like hell to get enough states called to get to 270 electoral votes," before Carter's concession. About ten minutes before Carter's scheduled press conference, ABC was able to call enough states with 270 electoral votes to project Reagan the winner. But those states included New York, which Mitofsky claims was so close, "they had no business calling it," and Maryland, which ABC incorrectly projected to go for Reagan. Following his usual cautious approach to projecting winners, Mitofsky did not get enough states to total 270 electoral votes until 10:20, more than two hours after NBC, a half hour after ABC, and twenty minutes after Carter's concession made the projection moot.

For the first time since Mitofsky had arrived at CBS, many at the network questioned his slowness. There was a "gnashing of teeth," he said. If NBC had come in first by using exit polls to project winners, why didn't CBS do the same? So the next year he did—in the New Jersey gubernatorial race. But he called the wrong winner.[4] It was much the same problem that he ran into thirteen years later in the 2004 presidential election—there was a strong Democratic bias in the numbers reported by the interviewers.

FOR THE NEXT four elections after Reagan's victory, the networks all used exit polls to call elections, when the results warranted it. If the exit polls showed a close race that was too close to call, the networks would wait for the vote count to project winners. No major problems surfaced in those years, though the cost of conducting the polls became prohibitive.

After the 1988 election, the networks called it quits with competing exit polls. They were just too expensive. ABC and CBS each offered proposals to the four networks (with the newcomer, CNN) for a joint network operation that would conduct the exit polls and project the winners. NBC did not offer a competing plan, but instead disbanded its election unit in anticipation of the consortium. After more than a year of often-contentious deliberations, CNN and NBC sided with CBS to form Voter Research and Surveys (VRS), headed by Mitofsky, who would implement the CBS proposal.

The decision did not sit well with the people at ABC, but they had little choice if they intended to save money on election night. Still, ABC's resentment of the CBS victory would soon unravel the apparent harmony that prevailed after VRS was formed.

One of the people most opposed to the CBS proposal was John Bly-denburgh, an ABC consultant since 1969 whose day job was teaching political science at Clark University.[5] He received his Ph.D. from the University of Rochester the same year he started working for ABC. At that time he was teaching at Rutgers University, where he met Don Herzberg, director of the Eagleton Institute, who was working with WABC in New York City on the 1969 New Jersey gubernatorial contest. Herzberg wanted to know: Could Blydenburgh project election winners from early vote returns? Blydenburgh was confident that he could and explained how—select a representative set of precincts which return their votes quickly, compare the results of this year's vote with previous years' gubernatorial elections to see the deviations in the Republican and Democratic votes, and use a little calculation to project what the vote will be in the rest of the state. "Most projections are really no-brainers," he told me many years later. But that year it was particularly easy, because William Cahill was expected to win handily, and he did. Blydenburgh's projection on the basis of his sample precincts was within two tenths of one percent of the actual vote ("I was lucky," he told me), which impressed ABC, where he has worked as a consultant on election and polling ever since.

In 1980, he and Jeff Alderman, an AP reporter who had joined ABC three years earlier to help with the election night projection, designed the exit poll operation that the network used on election night. Blydenburgh does not remember (but does not deny) that the analysts at ABC "raced like hell," as Mitofsky claimed, so they could call enough states to get the 270 electoral votes needed to project Reagan the winner before Carter conceded. Instead, Blydenburgh remembers that the analysts at ABC just called the races as they came. And they happened to beat CBS in the process.

What Blydenburgh remembers clearly is that the CBS exit poll model was substantially different from the ABC model. As part of the negotiations among the networks that led to the formation of VRS, Blydenburgh reviewed the CBS model in 1989. "It was completely incomprehensible," he told me. The statistical analyses were not clearly identified, and despite substantial effort, he could not get a clear documentation of the model from Murray Edelman, a long-time associate of Mitofsky. When the ABC executives asked Blydenburgh about the CBS model, "I told them it was a black box." You simply had to trust what CBS did, because there was no way to understand what the model did and thus what questions should be addressed. He thought that was not accidental. "One way to get power is to keep people ignorant," he said. And that's what he thought CBS and Mitofsky were trying to do.

As Blydenburgh saw it, the CBS "black box" was a statistically driven model, which essentially triggered a projection whenever the exit poll results and preliminary vote count showed a certain level of statistical significance. The ABC model, by contrast, provided raw data to the analysts, showing how the exit poll results and preliminary count compared with the vote distribution in previous years. There was no statistical "trigger," but instead a judgment that the analyst had to make about the likelihood that the winner would prevail, given the preliminary results.

Mitofsky's objection to the ABC proposal was that it was too loose, not driven by statistics. For him, it didn't make sense that ABC would be in charge of the consortium. "They're not big on methodology over there," he told me in 1991. "Read their methods. They're appalling."[6]

Blydenburgh's objection to the CBS model was that its statistically driven trigger point was shrouded in technical jargon that no one at CBS either could or would explain. Analysts would have to forego their own judgment for that of a mysterious black box. And that was not an appealing option.

DESPITE THE PERSISTENT differences of opinion, VRS was launched in 1990. It suffered many technical difficulties that first year, though to the average television viewer it was hard to detect any difference from other elections. On air, the anchors and reporters of each network pretended that the data came from their own network's operation, not acknowledging the consortium. All the projections made by each network originated from the VRS decision desks. Competition among the networks appeared dead.

Election Year 1992 proved even better for VRS, mostly in delivering the data on a timelier basis. And again, there was no competition. But there was as least one notable glitch. During the New Hampshire Republican Primary, VRS showed a tight, six-point contest between President George Bush and Patrick Buchanan, though Bush eventually won by sixteen points. The initial VRS results caused a major stir in the press, suggesting Bush was more vulnerable to Buchanan's candidacy than turned out to be the case.

Still, Murray Edelman, who later succeeded Mitofsky as director of the consortium's election night projection system, believes that VRS projections for the two elections of 1990 and 1992 constituted the ideal situation for the networks.[7] He acknowledges that in the early years of television, competition was intense on election night, because the network with the best coverage really benefited from increased viewership the rest of the year. But by the end of the 1980s, election night competition was not as crucial in the ratings wars among the networks. The goal of the networks at that time, he says, was to avoid embarrassment by coming in last, rather than to shine by coming in first. VRS provided that comfortable position for all the networks. It called the races, while the networks all took the credit. And no network beat the other.

But in 1994, ABC broke the implied covenant among the networks and got them all back on a collision course with democracy.

EVEN BEFORE ABC broke with the networks in 1994, some people within the networks had become disgruntled with Mitofsky and the operation of VRS. After the 1992 election, the board that governed VRS decided to combine NES (the network consortium that reported the vote count to VRS) with the exit poll operation under a new title, Voter News Service (VNS). The Fox network and the Associated Press also joined the consortium. Those appeared to be rather straightforward changes, but in the process the board also separated the directorship of the new consortium into two positions. Mitofsky was offered the position that would oversee the exit poll operation, as he had been doing, but given the whole employment package, it was an offer he could easily refuse. He quit to form his own exit poll business, Mitofsky International. Blydenburgh claims Mitofsky was essentially fired, because—among other things—he was such a difficult person to work with. In a later article, Rich Morin of *The Washington Post* echoed that view of Mitofsky by euphemistically referring to the pollster as a "formidable personality."[8] Mitofksy acknowledges that some people think of him as "difficult," but he says it's only because he won't compromise his standards. After observing him for literally hundreds of hours on many election nights under what for some would be severe stress, as well as seeing him in numerous other professional situations, I can say that rumors of his cantankerousness are highly exaggerated. He is often brusque, but inevitably quiet-spoken and humorous, with a dry wit that may be confused with a dour view of life, the opposite of his apparently indomitable optimism.

With Mitofsky out of the picture (temporarily, as it turned out), his long-time colleague Murray Edelman was put in charge of the exit poll operation, while Bob Flaherty of NES headed the vote-counting side of the organization. (This dual leadership structure persisted through the 1996 election, but by 1998, Bill Headline was the sole "executive director" of VNS. Edelman continued to oversee the exit poll operation with the title of "editorial director.")

ABC was never comfortable with the networks' decision to have CBS lead the consortium. It was no happier in 1994, now that Edelman was in charge, because he represented little substantive change from Mitofsky. Perhaps as a reflection of that continued disgruntle-ment, Carolyn Smith—director of ABC's election coverage— asked Blydenburgh at some point prior to the 1994 election if he could call the elections any faster than VNS. It's not clear who at ABC wanted the network to go head to head with VNS and the other networks, but Blydenburgh is convinced she was merely carrying out orders from above. "There's no way Carolyn would have done this on her own," he said. "She was too loyal." Though it may not have been her idea, she seemed to enjoy the prospect of battle.

In answer to Smith's question whether he could beat VNS at its own game, Blydenburgh said, "Sure!"

"How would you do it?" she asked, a sly smile beginning to form on her face.

He told her it really wasn't that difficult. Everyone had all of the data anyway (all the data at VRS, and later VNS, were displayed on com-puter screens simultaneously at the exit poll headquarters, as well as at each of the networks), so it was just a matter of analysis. He had been at VNS headquarters and seen the analysts there taking a lax attitude about calling the races. He would look at the data and see a race that was ready to call, but the analysts would be looking at something else or taking their time, not calling the races as soon as they could. "They were dragging their feet . . . they weren't really prepared . . . had no sense of getting it done in a timely fashion," he told her. What they needed at VNS was leadership, someone going around to check on the analysts, prodding them to look at the races that could be called. "But they had no leadership," he said.

After he finished his description of how he could call the races faster than VNS, Smith looked at him with what was now a broad smile. "Bly-denburgh," she said, "we're gonna kill them fuckers!"

And "kill" them they did.

Among the several races he called on Election Night 1994, Blyden-burgh projected George W. Bush the gubernatorial winner in Texas, Ollie North the loser of the U.S. Senate race in Virginia, and Mario

Cuomo the loser of the gubernatorial race in New York—all well before VNS made the same calls. CBS, CNN, and NBC all had to wait about an hour or so for VNS to catch up, since they didn't have anyone at their networks examining the data and making independent judgments. As Rich Morin of *The Washington Post* later wrote, "It was the polling equivalent of Pearl Harbor." Mitofsky complained, "The networks were blind-sided." Smith and Blydenburgh couldn't have been more pleased. "The peace thus broken, a range war began," Morin wrote.[9]

That was an ideal situation for Mitofsky, whose own exit poll business could not compete with the networks' consortium. Conducting exit polls and gathering the entire vote returns across the country was simply too expensive a project without major funding from the networks. But now that each network needed its own group of election night analysts, the job market suddenly took a turn for the better. Shortly after the 1994 election, Mitofsky received separate telephone calls from the executives at both CBS and CNN. Each network was forming its own decision team to compete with ABC and the other networks, and who better to make projections based on the VNS data than the man who designed the system. "I've often meant to send Carolyn Smith a 'thank you' note," Mitofsky told me years later in his inimitable gravely voice. "She's made me a lot of money over the years."[10] It was no doubt a delicious irony that the network that most wanted him ousted from VNS had been the source of his triumphant return. Mitofsky persuaded both CNN and CBS that they should hire him jointly, "because neither one could afford me on their own," he said. And they bought his argument that neither network really competed with the other. CNN had its own cable niche (Fox only came into existence in October 1996), and CBS's main rivals were ABC and NBC.

IN ELECTION YEAR 1996, the networks were statistically armed and ready for war. Yet, oddly enough, the networks' decision teams at first appeared rather cautious, occasionally calling a race faster than VNS, but most of the time following the lead of VNS's editorial director, Murray Edelman. But by Election Night 2000, Edelman was worried. "The networks were becoming more aggressive in calling the races," he told me. He had noticed that aggressiveness in 1998 and again during the primaries in 2000. So, a week before the general election, he sent a memo to all of the networks' decision desks, warning them of the problems in data gathering. He was especially concerned that later in the evening and early the next morning, as projections were based less on exit polls and more on the actual vote count, that analysts would put too much trust in the numbers displayed on the screen. "I gave several examples where [in the past] the vote count was off by as much as half a percent, even when more than 99 percent of the vote was counted."[11]

In the case of Florida, with a total of about six million votes in the 2000 election, that meant a margin of even 30,000 votes in Florida would have to be treated as suspect, and not a sufficient reason for calling an election—a fact the network decision teams already knew, but which, at 2:15 the morning after Election Night 2000, they simply ignored.

Had John Ellis paid more attention to the memo and less attention to his cousin Jebbie, Fox would not have called the election for George W. Bush. And had the other network decision teams paid more attention to the memo than to the Fox call, the networks would not have followed Fox like the proverbial lemmings off a cliff. For Mitofsky, the genuine guru who had designed the election night projection system and was widely recognized as the "pioneer and leader in the field,"[12] Election Night 2000 would turn out to be the worst election of his professional life.

We largely discount the Decision Team's [Warren Mitofsky's and Joe Lenski's] insistence that time pressures were not a problem in calling Florida prematurely.

—Television's Performance on Election Night 2000:
A Report for CNN, *January 29, 2001*

The competitive drive to be first played a powerful role [in the bad calls on Election Night 2000].

—*Tom Johnson, chairman and CEO of CNN News Group, January 29, 2001*

3

"Hell to Pay"

The first sign that Election Night 2000 would become what veteran pollster Warren Mitofsky later called "the worst election I can remember" came at exactly nine o'clock.[1] He and his partner, Joe Lenski, a 1980 graduate of Princeton, and several other assistants and I were all peering at computer screens in a windowless room in the CBS building on 235 West Fifty-seventh Street in New York City, a block and a half east of the Hudson River. The information that streamed into their computers originated from Voter News Service (VNS), located at the southern tip of Manhattan in one of the World Trade Center buildings. Formed by the five major networks (ABC, CBS, CNN, Fox, and NBC) and the Associated Press, VNS was responsible for overseeing the most extensive election night analysis operation in the world.

Throughout the day, VNS had conducted exit polls in selected precincts all across the country, asking voters as they left the voting booths which candidates they had voted for and why. In addition, VNS had been collecting actual vote counts in selected precincts once the polls had closed, to see how closely the exit poll results mirrored the real vote. All of that information was fed into a central computer at VNS headquarters, and into complex statistical models developed over a decade earlier, which would predict the winner in each of the ninety-six contests being covered—the presidential race in all fifty states and Washington, D.C., plus eleven gubernatorial and thirty-four U.S. Senate races. The networks used the data not just to call the races, but also to interpret the election results, to explain to viewers what issues were important to voters, and how those issues influenced their decisions.

Mitofsky and Lenski were the co-directors of the joint CBS/CNN decision team, responsible for analyzing the VNS data and telling the two networks when they should project winners in each of the states. Four other decision teams were distributed throughout the city, one each for ABC, NBC, Fox, and the Associated Press. I was there because earlier I had told Mitofsky that I was interested in writing a book about the 2000 election from a polling perspective, and he suggested that I observe what it was like on election night with the exit polls. I had first met Mitofsky in 1991, when I interviewed him for my book *The Super Pollsters*.[2] We maintained professional contact over the years through the American Association for Public Opinion Research. I was delighted, of course, to accept his invitation. With the election expected to be close, it promised to be an exciting night. No one could have anticipated how momentous it would actually be.

On the computer, the election night projection system provided seventeen "pages" of data for each race, a total of over 1,600 hundred computer screens that a decision team could access as it considered whether the statistical models could accurately predict the winner. The mission of each decision team: call each race as quickly as possible, *without making a miscall*. The goal was to beat the other networks and VNS itself, which had the formal responsibility for calling the races. Once VNS called the race, usually all of the networks would follow. But if the network decision team could beat the VNS call, and the competitor networks, so much the better.

At 9:00 P.M. on Election Night 2000, Mitofsky and Lenski were switching back and forth between the pages (what the analysts called "decision screens") covering the presidential contests in Louisiana, Ohio, and Minnesota, as they considered whether to call a winner in any of those races. Lenski's colleague, Larry Rosen, told the team leaders to switch to page 2 of the Florida presidential data, which displayed the votes according to five geographic "strata" in the state—the Miami area, the rest of the south, the Tampa Bay area, the central area, and the north. What Mitofsky and Lenski saw made them wince.

The page displayed two predictive models, one based solely on the exit poll, the VPA model, and the other based on the exit poll supplemented by actual vote count, the Core model. At the time, the VNS system estimated that 24 percent of the total vote had been counted. If the exit poll was correct, both the VPA and the Core models should show essentially the same figures. And, in fact, in four of the strata, the two models were almost identical, suggesting the exit poll in those areas was indeed quite accurate. What troubled the team leaders was the other stratum, the Tampa Bay area, which, according to the Core model, had 57 percent of the vote for Bush and 41 percent for Gore. In the exit poll model, the numbers were almost perfectly reversed: 57 percent for Gore and 40 percent for Bush. Then Lenski noticed the statewide summary. The exit poll model showed Gore ahead overall by 53 percent to 45 percent. The Core model showed the exact opposite, Bush winning by 53 percent to 45 percent. Something was wrong. Big time!

Only an hour and ten minutes earlier, on page 1 of the Florida presidential data, the best predictive model showed Gore with 51.4 percent of the vote to 46.2 percent for Bush—a difference of 5.2 percentage points. At that time, only 4 percent of the vote was in, but all the actual vote data were consistent with the exit poll results. Statistically, the model said, there was only one chance in 200 that Gore was not the winner. That was the decision point, and Mitofsky was about to call the race when the television monitor on the wall showed that NBC had just projected Gore the winner in Florida.

"Shit!" Mitofsky said, a rueful expression on his face. "They beat us by two seconds." Then he got on the phone with CNN and CBS and said, "Call Florida for Gore."

Now, sixty-eight minutes later, as Lenski showed Mitofsky the "weird" numbers in Florida's third stratum and the reversal of the statewide summary, the veteran pollster felt a vague foreboding. Of more than 2,000 calls he had made in previous exit polls, only six times had he made a call and then been forced to retract it. In a presidential race, he had miscalled only once, projecting Dukakis the winner in Illinois in 1988. But the race there had not been decisive. Dukakis would have lost the presidency even if he had won Illinois. This situation was different. Since Mitofsky had called Gore in Florida, other states had been decided for Gore and Bush. Now, as he said, "If Florida flips, Bush wins!"

The First Rescission—"Real Trouble"

9:14 Mitofsky gets on the phone with Murray Edelman, the editorial director of VNS, a former assistant who had worked with Mitofsky since 1967, when they both went to work at CBS. "Murray, we may have a little problem in Florida." Edelman says he will check the numbers.

9:15 Mitofsky makes a final check of the Ohio data and gets on the phone with CNN and CBS: "Bush in Ohio." He continues perusing the computer screens in other states.

9:16 An assistant who was watching the television monitors announces that ABC has called Bush in Louisiana. Mitofsky looks at me and smiles. He called the race at 9:00, when the polls closed.

9:19 NBC calls Ohio for Bush. Another victory for the CNN/CBS team. Only four minutes. But a win is a win.

9:21 Mitofsky smiles again when ABC calls Gore in Pennsylvania. Mitofsky called that race at 8:49. He wins by a full half hour.

9:23 VNS calls Bush in Louisiana, twenty-three minutes after

Mitofsky. But that's not a big victory. VNS has to be more cautious. If one of the networks makes a miscall, that affects only that network's viewers. But if VNS gives its stamp of approval and later has to retract a call, that affects all the networks and the whole country. Were Mitofsky and Lenski the decision team for VNS, they might be much more cautious.

9:29 The model in Ohio shows a closer race than it did when Mitofsky called the winner fourteen minutes ago. If the model had shown the race this close earlier, he would not have called a winner. I ask him if that bothers him. He grins. "Don't be concerned about a reversal yet!" Later, in a memo to CNN, he and Lenski would propose more conservative standards for calling races. If those standards had been in effect tonight, Mitofsky and Lenski would not have called Ohio until 10:10, almost an hour later than when they actually called it. Still, Ohio will end up in Bush's column as projected.

9:30 Mitofsky is on the phone with Edelman again, but the VNS editorial director cannot explain the errors in the third stratum in Florida. There actually appear to be two sources of error in the Florida data, one in the third stratum and another in the fifth stratum, which includes Duval County. Vote reports in Duval County show Gore receiving 98 percent of the vote with 6 percent of the precincts reporting. Edelman tells Mitofsky he will try to block the Duval County vote from the model, but seems uncertain as to whether he can succeed. "I can take it out, but they will keep sending it," he says.

9:31 NBC calls Minnesota for Gore, but Mitofsky and Lenski are not convinced. They advise CNN and CBS against a call. Mitofsky pages through the data for Florida.

9:33 ABC calls Minnesota for Gore, but still Mitofsky and Lenski resist. Their focus is on the Florida numbers.

9:37 Mitofsky gets on the phone with CNN and CBS. "Gore in Minnesota," he says.

9:38   A note from VNS pops up on the screen about the data in Florida. Edelman has succeeded. The message reads: "We are canceling the vote in CNTY 16, Duval County. Vote is strange." Mitofsky shakes his head. "This is real trouble." With that vote removed, the race is even. Florida should never have been called for Gore.

9:41   Mitofsky talks on the phone with Kathy Frankovic at CBS, his former assistant when he was director of the CBS polling operation, a job Frankovic now holds. Also on the phone is Tom Hannon at CNN, the network's political director. Mitofsky explains the VNS problem with Florida.

"We believe there are data mistakes," he says. "If the county data get corrected, then Bush may be the winner. Both VPA and Core have mistaken data . . . yeah, two separate errors." He tells them that Edelman is reluctant to rescind the call because he claims "we don't have enough information right now to pull it back . . . we could look silly . . . " Mitofsky is not at all happy with Edelman's decision.

This is not what the executives want to hear. If they have to rescind the call, it will be a major embarrassment. The only redeeming aspect is that VNS and all of the other networks have also called Florida for Gore.

9:43   ABC calls New Mexico for Gore.

Mitofsky is still talking with Frankovic and Hannon; he tells them the vote count shows Duval County with 98 percent of the vote for Gore, which has to be a mistake. Four years ago Clinton got only 44 percent. Besides, no one ever gets 98 percent of the vote! (In fact, Gore eventually ends up with 41 percent of the Duval County vote.)

NBC calls New Mexico for Gore.

Frankovic and Hannon ask if they should rescind the Florida call. "We need more information from Murray," Mitofsky says.

9:47   An associate points to the televisions on the opposite wall, where George W. Bush is being interviewed. Mitofsky says over the phone, "Bush is not conceding Florida."

Lenski and Mitofsky review the screens for Florida. The discrepancies can't be explained. Mitofsky picks up the open phone to VNS and speaks to one of Edelman's associates. "We are close to rescinding the call in Florida. You'd better get Murray over here." A moment later Edelman is on the phone. "Murray, we've got to talk . . ."

9:50 An assistant asks Lenski, "Are we ready to call New Mexico?" By now, two of the networks have already made the call for Gore. "No," Lenski says. "We have a nuclear bomb ready to go off."

9:54 After telling Frankovic and Hannon, Mitofsky sends an electronic note to other members, rescinding the Florida call for CNN and CBS with the understated explanation, "We don't entirely trust all the information we have in from VNS." Edelman and Mitofsky argue about the call, but Edelman will not rescind. There's still at least a 50–50 chance Gore is the winner. Edelman says again he doesn't want VNS to look silly. Mitofsky acknowledges that Gore could still win, but the models show neither candidate the definite winner at this point. The public is being misled. "It's irresponsible not to rescind," says Mitofsky. Later, Republicans will scream that the miscall in Florida, projecting Gore the winner, depressed Republican vote turnout in other parts of the country. No credible evidence for this type of assertion is ever produced, but that isn't the reason Mitofsky has decided to rescind the call now. His reason is more basic: the call was wrong, even if it turns out to be right in the long run.

10:05 Following Mitofsky's rescission, ABC and Fox have also rescinded the Florida call, but both NBC—which called Florida first—and VNS still have Gore the winner. It's logical that a network might want to delay a rescission in the hopes that the outcome will eventually be right. But this state is too crucial to the election to allow the networks to say it is in the Gore column when the data don't support that at this time.

10:15 VNS finally rescinds the call; NBC follows. The VNS message reads: "We are retracting our call in FL because we don't have the confidence we did and we are still examining the absentee vote."

10:19 Mitofsky calls New Mexico for Gore. Later this decision will add to Mitofsky's woes of election 2000, as the race in that state was so close it took days before Gore was finally declared the winner. The problem was an error in the vote count, but it will be seen as another VNS and network mistake.

Earlier in the evening, CBS anchor Dan Rather had assured his audience that when CBS called an election, viewers could "pretty much take it to the bank, book it, that that's true." He reassured his audience that CBS was interested in accuracy. "Let's get one thing straight from the get-go. We would rather be last in reporting returns than to be wrong." Throughout the evening, as the network anchors made each call, they acted as though they alone had data supporting that decision. Now, with an egregious embarrassment in the making, Rather was eager to share the blame. He told the CBS audience, "Based on what we believed, and most other people believed at the time—I know of nobody who didn't believe it—. . . it turns out some of the data is suspect."

Also earlier in the evening on CNN, Bill Schneider had assured his audience of the accuracy of CNN calls. The conservative CNN commentator, Mary Matalin, challenged the accuracy of the Florida call at the time it was made, suggesting the absentee ballots would tip the election in Bush's favor. Schneider replied, "Well, when we do call the state, we've taken the absentee ballot count into account." He did not know at the time that the number of absentee ballots had been woefully underestimated by VNS. "When we call the state," he said, "we're pretty sure that state is going to go for the winner."

Now, on CNN, Jeff Greenfield was talking when the co-anchor, Bernard Shaw, said, "Stand by, stand by . . . CNN right now is moving our earlier declaration of Florida back to the too-close-to-call column."

Greenfield: "Oh, waiter . . . one order of crow."

Schneider: "One order of crow. Yes."

As the evening progressed, the Bush margin in Florida continued to increase. By 10:40, with 60 percent of the estimated vote already counted, Bush led by 190,000 votes. On a conference call with Kathy Frankovic at CBS and Tom Hannon at CNN, Mitofsky reiterated what he had said earlier.

"The outcome will hinge on Florida. It looks like it's going to be Bush. . . . Florida will tip the balance."

A few minutes later, when new numbers increased the lead, he said with even more conviction, "Now Bush is going to win." It was decided.

In the meantime, Mitofsky and Lenski continued to project winners in other contests. At 12:40, they were the first to call the U.S. Senate race in Washington State for Democratic challenger Maria Cantwell over Republican incumbent Slade Gorton. They made the call because the exit poll showed Cantwell up by ten points, and absentee vote totals showed an even split for the Republican and Democratic candidates. As it turns out, the report on absentee votes included Election Day results, and the exit poll itself had a Democratic bias. That race would not be decided for days, and should not have been called on election night.

At 12:45 new worrisome information from 2,500 miles away. With 91 percent of the vote counted in New Mexico, Gore was up by only 4,600 votes, with 70,000 absentees to be counted. And a majority would likely go for Bush. But by what margin? This could be a mistake. "But . . . it's probably safe," Mitofsky said. At it turned out, he was wrong. The race was so close it would take weeks of more counting before Gore was finally certified on December 5 as the winner of New Mexico's five electoral votes.[3] The race should never have been called.

Back in Florida, a few minutes before midnight, Bush was up by 110,000 votes, with an estimated million or so votes to be counted. Much of the vote was still out in Broward and Miami-Dade counties, where Gore was doing well. So, the margin would decrease, but probably not below the 20,000 level Mitofsky estimated. And this didn't include the overseas absentee ballots. When I asked Mitofsky how he thought the absentee vote would go, he said, "Oh, it's going to be for

Bush. I've never seen absentee votes come in the other way." Overseas absentees included upscale people living in Europe and the military, two groups that tend to be Republican. If Bush were to break even in the Election Day vote, he would win because of the absentees.

At 1:07 the new estimate had Bush winning by 30,000 votes, plus the margin from the absentees. I asked Mitofsky why he didn't call Florida if he was so sure of the margin.

"Do you want to call the president of the United States on the basis of 30,000 votes? Right now Bush leads by 65,000 votes and at three in the morning he'll likely have a 30,000-vote margin. Are you comfortable with that? I'm not. Vote counts are not 100 percent sure. Some end-of-night vote counts are off by at least one point . . . the counts are reported by the media . . . and they make mistakes."

At the time, I didn't know that Mitofsky was parroting a memo that Murray Edelman had sent the previous week to all of the networks and AP, warning the decision teams to be careful about the vote counts. Ironically, had Mitofsky followed his own advice only an hour later, he would not have made the second miscall. The total vote was expected to be close to six million votes. According to Mitofsky's own warning, even a 60,000 vote margin would not be enough to make a comfortable projection, because of the possibility of a one-percentage-point error in the total estimated six million Florida votes.

Second Florida Miscall . . . Following Fox Off the Deep End

1:57 Mitofsky calls the Missouri Senate race for Democrat Mel Carnahan, who died in an airplane accident a few days before the election. The governor has promised to appoint Carnahan's widow should voters choose the Democrat against incumbent Republican Senator John Ashcroft. Fox has already called the race.

2:05 Fox calls Iowa for Gore.

2:06 Mitofsky tells CNN and CBS: Gore in Iowa.

2:07 VNS shows Bush ahead in Florida by 29,000 votes, with 96 percent of the vote in. The Core estimate shows Bush up by only 0.2 percent—way too close to call the winner.

2:12 Something strange has happened with the Florida data, though it will not be noticed until too late. VNS now shows Bush ahead by over 51,000 votes, still with 96 percent of the vote in. Only 4,000 more votes have been tabulated in the past five minutes, but Bush's lead has jumped by 22,000 votes. This error would prove fatal in the pending miscall.

The strange numbers come from Volusia County, whose vote reports were read into the database at 2:08, just four minutes ago. Gore's total in the county drops by more than 10,000 (from 82,619 to 72,152) while Bush's total increases by almost 10,000 votes (from 63,265 to 73,146). Clearly, something is amiss. Either the previous data or the current data are in error, and the analysts need to determine immediately which are correct. Such a dramatic change should be carefully checked, and Edelman should be notified personally about the change. But a VNS supervisor approves the new numbers without notifying Edelman, and they are entered into the system unnoticed by analysts who are focusing on the many other races still undecided. The error will not be discovered for forty minutes. Not until after the biggest miscall in half a century.

2:15 Gore is down by about 51,000 votes in Florida with an estimated 179,000 votes to be counted. Mitofsky estimates that Gore will need 63 percent of the remaining outstanding vote, but can make up at most about 20,000 votes total in Palm Beach, Miami-Dade, and Broward counties.[4] "If the numbers are correct," Mitofsky says, "Bush will win Florida." That caution is prescient. "If the numbers are correct."

2:16 Mitofsky is considering whether to call the race for Bush, the 1 percent error warning apparently not even a factor in his calculation.

As Edelman will later observe, although analysts know of potential errors in the data, at a certain point the numbers take on a life of their own. The logic of what the numbers show overrides the possibility that they could just be wrong. Mitofsky makes another check of the counties. Seconds later Fox calls Florida for Bush! "Fox has an agenda, don't forget," Mitofsky says and continues his review.

2:17   "NBC just called Florida," someone announces. "We'll do it, too!" Mitofsky says. Twenty-two seconds later, CBS and CNN announce Bush the winner in Florida and the next president of the United States.

After making the call, Mitofsky says, "Fox did well tonight. ABC bringing up the rear." He grins. He likes to beat ABC. That network started the competition in 1994, fooling all the other networks that had relied solely on VNS projections. So, it was always nice to beat ABC at its own game.

But Fox would not be given credit for a job well done. And in less than a hundred minutes, Mitofsky would rue his rush to judgment.

By 2:20 in the morning, every network had declared in flashing lights, "George Walker Bush, 43rd President of the United States." No one anticipated that this call could possibly be wrong. The ultimate faith in the projection was best expressed by Cokie Roberts on ABC, when the anchor, Peter Jennings, asked her, "This is it?"

"Yes. It's been a very cautious night, Peter, after the initial first bad call. And so I think that, unlike other times, instead of rushing to make calls—here it is, what, 2:30 in the morning?—so this is likely to be it. Yes."

In Austin and in Nashville early in the morning of November 8, reporters waited for the candidates to come forth and publicly accept the verdict of the American people. But that would not happen for weeks.

The Second Rescission—
Not an Egg on Their Face, but an Omelet

2:50 The decision screen shows that in the past ten minutes 8,000 more votes have been counted statewide, but Bush's margin is now 16,000 votes smaller! Clearly, some correction has been made to the vote count, but there is no notification of the correction. Mitofsky and Lenski do not notice the discrepancy. Nor, apparently, does anyone on the other decision teams, nor anyone at VNS. Only a later review of the decision screens will make clear what has just happened. At 2:48, a corrected vote count from Volusia County was entered into the database. The new figures gave Gore almost 25,000 more votes than the number posted at 2:08, and the new report also gave Bush 9,000 more votes. No one notified Edelman— nor any of the networks—that a correction was being made.

3:00 Bush's lead is now down to 11,000, far below what Mitofsky had earlier estimated. But with only 25,000 votes yet to be counted, Mitofsky thinks Florida still looks solid for Bush. Gore will need 71 percent of the remaining vote to catch up. But Mitofsky is uncomfortable with the drop. "We are depending on this count to be correct." He would be even more uncomfortable if he knew about the data correction in Volusia County.

3:03 David Schenfeld, Mitofsky's computer wizard, surfs the Web and ends up on the Web site of Florida's secretary of state. That site shows that only 4,600 votes separate Gore from Bush, with 99.7 percent of the vote counted. Tight. But still likely for Bush, again assuming no major error in the vote count.

3:10 The bombshell! The Florida's secretary of state Web site shows 99.8 percent of the vote counted, and just a 569-vote margin! "There's going to be hell to pay on this one," Mitofsky says. By contrast, the VNS decision screen still shows Bush with close to an 11,000-vote margin, and 21,000 votes to be counted. Either the Florida secretary of state or VNS is wrong.

3:15 Mitofsky talks with Edelman, pointing out the discrepancies between VNS and the Florida secretary of state's office. Edelman says he will check and get back to them. In the meantime, Mitofsky and Lenski print out the vote totals for each county as listed on the secretary of state's office Web site and compare them with the VNS numbers. The numbers vary significantly in seven counties. The discrepancies are reported to VNS, and the VNS numbers are corrected.

3:27 VNS sends a message to its subscribers. "Florida—the Sec of State Web site has a much narrower margin for Bush. We are comparing county by county trying to determine discrepancies."

3:40 The VNS screen now shows Bush with a 6,000-vote lead and 16,000 votes left to be counted. Gore needs 68 percent of the remaining vote to catch Bush. Most of the outstanding vote is in Broward County, where the precincts whose votes have already been counted show Gore getting 67.8 percent of the vote. Now, even VNS shows a toss-up!

3:51 Back on the secretary of state's Web site, Bush's margin has increased from less than 600 to 1,200 votes. But the margin is too small. Vote-counting error alone could wipe out that margin.

3:55 Mitofsky is on the line with Kathy Frankovic at CBS. He wants to rescind the call for both networks. "Kathy, please wait until Tom [Hannon of CNN] gets back on the line."

3:59 Mitofsky: "Make sure Tom knows about it, Kathy—we're taking it down."

IN THE NEXT several minutes, the other networks followed Mitofsky's lead. Ironically, VNS and AP had never called Florida for Bush, not trusting the data, but trusting Edelman's memo that vote-counting errors alone can amount to more than half a percent of the vote. Yet, VNS would be pilloried for making two miscalls on Florida in the same night. Had all the networks followed VNS, keeping the Florida race as too close to call, the brouhaha over the election night calls might never have happened, or at the very least would have been less rancorous.

After assuring his audience of the special accuracy of the CBS calls, Dan Rather exhorted his viewers not to blame him for this second blunder. "I'm always reminded of those west Texas saloons where they had a sign that says, 'Please don't shoot the piano player; he's doing the best he can.' That's been pretty much the case here tonight over this election."

On NBC, Tom Brokaw had his own metaphor. "We don't just have egg on our face. We have an omelet all over our suit."

You believe it was all coincidence that Fox, where Governor Bush's first cousin worked and helped make a decision having talked several times that night with . . . his first cousins, that [Fox] went first and the other networks afterwards—that's total coincidence?

—Congressman Sherrod Brown (D) Ohio,
at the congressional hearings, February 14, 2001

I can't imagine it being anything else.

—Ben Wattenberg, senior fellow, American Enterprise Institute,
at the congressional hearings, February 14, 2001

It was just the three of us guys handing the phone back and forth, me with the numbers, one of them a governor, the other the president-elect. Now, that was cool.

—John Ellis, head of Fox decision team on
Election Night 2000, November 20, 2000

Mr. Ellis is the first cousin of President George W. Bush and Governor Jeb Bush. We at Fox News do not discriminate against people because of their family connections.

—Roger Ailes, chairman and CEO of
Fox News Network, February 14, 2001

4

The "Cool" Cousins

If anyone could have stopped Fox's rush to judgment the morning after Election Day, it was Cynthia Talkov, the thirty-seven-year-old Berkeley-trained statistician who sat next to John Ellis for thirteen hours of Fox's election coverage.[1] The fact that she didn't stop the call has plagued her ever since. She believes that the Fox call triggered the calls by the other networks, erroneously giving the impression that George W. Bush was the winner, influencing Al Gore to concede the race prematurely, and setting up a political environment after the election that clearly favored Bush over Al Gore. But her distress over the Fox projection was only tangentially related to the possibility that the miscall might have been one of the crucial elements in Bush's improbable victory in 2000. She was mostly devastated because she was the statistician with the responsibility for stopping any calls not supported by the data. And she knew it was not data that spurred Ellis to call the election for Bush, but the exhortations of George W. Bush's own brother, Jeb Bush.

At a little after two in the morning, after being on the phone with the Florida governor for many minutes, as he had been many times that evening, Ellis suddenly announced to his decision team, "Jebbie says we got it! Jebbie says we got it!" At that point he asked if any of the other members of the team objected to calling the race for Bush. John Gorman, president of Opinion Dynamics, the polling firm con- tracted to do Fox's regular public opinion polling, offered no objection. Nor did Arnon Mishkin, partner in the Boston Consulting Group and Ellis' former associate at the NBC News election unit in the mid-1980s. The fourth member of the team, Cynthia Talkov, the only statistician on the team, did not support making any projection at the time, "because I think it was too close to call based solely on the VNS num- bers." Still, she said nothing when Ellis asked the team if anyone objected to calling Florida for Bush. If Ellis wanted to call the race on the basis of outside information, even if from the brother of one of the candidates, that was his prerogative. In the end, she felt, the actual vote count would make any network call irrelevant. At the time it never occurred to her that the Fox call, and subsequent calls by the other net- works, might help to prevent a fair and complete vote count from ever taking place.

ELLIS WAS THE de facto head of the Fox decision team, hired for the 1998 election and again for the 2000 election. He was so passionately biased in favor of his first cousin George W. Bush that in a July 3, 1999, op-ed for the *Boston Globe,* he explained why he had to stop writing columns about the 2000 presidential campaign: "I am loyal to my cousin, Gov. George Bush. I put that loyalty ahead of my loyalty to any- one outside my immediate family. . . . There is no way for you to know if I am telling you the truth about George W. Bush's presidential cam- paign because in my case, my loyalty goes to him and not to you."[2] That sentiment didn't disqualify him from being Fox's exit-poll guru; in fact, it may have been his major qualification. Later, Roger Ailes, chairman and CEO of Fox, would tell a congressional committee, "Mr. Ellis is the first cousin of President George W. Bush and Governor Jeb Bush. We at Fox News do not discriminate against people because of their family connections." He went on to state, incorrectly as it turns out, that Ellis "has almost 23 years of experience in calling elections."[3] Ellis also claimed in a post-election article for *Inside* magazine that "having worked at the NBC News Election Unit for 11 years (1978–1989) and having covered politics for most of my adult life (from 1994 to 1999 as a columnist at the *Boston Globe*), I knew my way around election results"[4] What Ellis didn't acknowledge, and apparently Ailes didn't recognize, was that Ellis's work at NBC had little or nothing to do with actually "calling elections," and that Ellis had little understanding of the statistical methods used for projecting winning candidates based on exit polls and partial vote returns.

Despite his public preening, Ellis himself seemed to recognize his limitations. He made sure that Talkov was sitting next to him throughout Election Day and night, describing her in the post-election article for *Inside* magazine as his "statistical wizard." "Her VNS experience was invaluable to us. We needed someone who knew the system inside out, knew the details and pitfalls of each and every estimator on our screens, and knew exactly who to call when we had questions that could only be answered by VNS employees."[5]

For her part, Talkov was not exactly thrilled to be working with the Fox team that evening. When she had worked previously on election nights, the teams had all consisted of well-trained people on the exit poll models, who worked with each other, sharing their interpretations and treating each other as the friendly colleagues they were. In 1990 and 1992 at VRS, she had worked with Warren Mitofsky and Murray Edelman. In 1994, after VRS morphed into VNS and Mitofsky formed his own exit poll operation, Talkov left CBS to work with Mitofsky International. That year, she worked with Mitofsky as he competed with VNS, and in the next couple of years she helped him conduct numerous exit polls in other countries, to include Russia and Mexico. In 1996, the same year that Mitofsky was hired (along with Joe Lenski) to form the combined decision team for CBS and CNN, Talkov went to work for a polling firm called Opinion Dynamics, so she could get back to the Boston area. During that year, she also took vacation time so she could work as a consultant with Murray Edelman, the editorial director at VNS, to call election results on primary election nights and on election night itself.

But now, in 2000, as in the 1998 midterm elections, she felt obligated to work for Fox because of her employment with Opinion Dynamics, Fox's polling firm. Unlike her previous experience with exit poll operations, the three men on the team were not well trained on the statistical models, and more distressing, they seemed little interested in having her explain how the models worked. Perhaps most resistant to hearing anything from her was John Gorman, president of Opinion Dynamics, her employer for four years until she resigned shortly before the 2000 election. Ellis would later write of Gorman that he was "the most senior member" of the Fox decision team, and "arguably one of the best pollsters in the country."[6] On what grounds Ellis would be able to say that is a mystery. It's not that Gorman wasn't a competent pollster, it's just that the criteria for identifying the best in the profession are hardly self-evident. Moreover, Gorman's experience was irrelevant to using the election night models for calling elections, a completely different enterprise from public opinion polling. He had never been trained on the VNS models before he joined the Fox decision team in 1998. Even in 2000, according to Talkov, Gorman—as well as Ellis and Mishkin—had little understanding of what many of the numbers on the computer screens conveyed about the election.

The decision team's lack of knowledge was so manifest during the primary season that Talkov asked Murray Edelman of VNS to come over to Fox and explain some of the rudimentary elements of the exit poll models to Gorman, Mishkin, and Ellis. She warned Edelman that, at least to her, they had been unwilling to listen, maybe because she was a woman, or because she was young and worked for Gorman. She thought Edelman might have better luck. But after Edelman went to Fox and made his presentation, he told Talkov, "My God, you were right!" They had been as dismissive toward him as they had been toward her. In a 2005 interview, Edelman said his most vivid memory was of Ellis, who was "so arrogant, as though he knew it all. When I talked with him, I thought 'Whoa!'— he was so confident, but knew so little."[7]

By Election Day 2000, Talkov had given up any notion that she might help the three men on the decision team understand the data displays on the computer screens. Gorman and Mishkin were across the room from Ellis and her, each with his own computer screen. They would occasionally come over to where she and Ellis were sitting and "jibber jabber away," as she termed it, about how the election was going in one state or another, but instead of trying to explain to them what the data really showed, she just ignored their mindless chatter. Besides, this was her last stint with Fox; all she had to do was make sure that none of the calls that evening was wrong.

As for Ellis, he spent much of his time talking with George W. or Jeb Bush by phone. She had first become aware of Ellis's conversations with his cousins during the New Hampshire primary, when she picked up Ellis' phone while he was away from the desk. A voice asked to speak with Ellis. When she asked who was calling, she was startled to hear, "George Bush." On Election Day 2000, from sometime in the afternoon through the rest of the day and evening and into the next morning, Ellis was often on the phone with one or both of his cousins, talking with them about the exit poll numbers and the likelihood that Bush would win the election. At the same time, Gorman and Mishkin were often on the phone to people at the Democratic National Committee. For Talkov, it was a world turned upside down. At VRS and VNS, there had been no contact between political operatives and Mitofsky or Edelman or any other people working with the exit polls. Certainly, no one would have considered talking directly with any candidate and discussing electoral strategy. The decision team members were supposed to be objective analysts, influenced by the data, not by discussions with partisans who may have had an interest in the elections being called one way or the other. Talkov was appalled.

BY SIX THAT evening, when Fox began its news coverage, Talkov and Ellis had identified all the races that were expected to be closely contested and had listed them by poll-closing times. The first calls would not be until seven, the earliest closing time for any state, which also included most of Florida. But no one called Florida at seven. The exit poll data showed Gore ahead, but his lead was not great enough for the models to project him the winner beyond a reasonable doubt (identified statistically as only one chance in two hundred of being wrong). The analysts would wait for the computer models to incorporate actual vote counts before considering a projection.

Although precincts in Florida's panhandle did not close their polls until eight, vote counting in the rest of the state began immediately after their seven o'clock closings. Those early vote tallies were read into the computer models, and by 7:45 they suggested that the exit polls had been fairly accurate. In fact, the actual vote count showed that if the polls were off at all, they had underestimated Gore's lead over Bush. At 7:49 NBC News called the state for Gore, followed immediately by Mitofsky's and Lenski's call for CBS and CNN, which got on the air at 7:50. Fox called it two minutes later.

In his article for *Inside* magazine, Ellis writes that before Fox made the Florida call, Mishkin and Gorman were still "dubious" about the numbers showing Gore the winner. If so, the reservations were not because of the statistical models. No one looking at the data could have come to any other conclusion. It was like the perfect storm of mistakes that led to the miscall.

First, there was a bad sample of precincts. The statistical experts at VNS had chosen the sample of precincts around the state using approved random sampling techniques, but there is always a small chance that any sample will not be representative of the larger population. In more than three decades of conducting exit polls, Mitofsky said he had witnessed only one other time when a bad sample led to a miscall.

Then, there was a slight miscalculation in the models themselves. They are programmed to measure what statisticians refer to as the "standard error of the estimate," which calculates how well any sample can represent the larger population. The model showed that Gore was up by just over seven percentage points, with a standard error of less than three points. That meant there was less than 1 chance in 200 that the actual vote count would actually have Bush winning. But after the election, some sharp-eyed statisticians noticed that there was a slight bias in the calculation of the standard error. When only a small proportion of the actual vote count was included in the model, the standard error was smaller than it should be, though that bias gradually disappeared as more data were added. Had that bias been discovered and corrected before the election, no call for Gore would have been made.

That mistaken calculation had apparently been in the models at least since the networks had joined forces in 1988, but it was always so small it had never before contributed to a miscall. For the 2004 operation, the formulas in the models were changed to produce a more accurate standard error.

Finally, the models in the Florida race assumed that the pattern of voting for president in 2000 would be similar to the pattern of voting in the 1998 gubernatorial race, when Jeb Bush won reelection as governor. As a constant check on status of the contest, the models would calculate how much the votes in each precinct for George W. Bush in 2000 differed from the votes that Jeb Bush received in 1998. The purpose of this comparison is to guard against wild differences between the pattern of voting, which could suggest an error in the vote count. For example, if Jeb Bush won 57 percent of the vote in a given precinct, but now George W. Bush was getting only 20 percent of the vote, that would raise a red flag.

As it turns out, the pattern of voting in the 1998 gubernatorial election was not the best race for this comparison, because the state issues that influenced the vote that year differed from the national issues that influenced the vote in 2000. A better comparison would have been with the presidential race of 1996. When the initial exit poll results were compared with several recent statewide races in Florida, the models showed that both statewide races—the 1996 presidential and the 1998 gubernatorial contests—correlated highly with the 2000 vote. Which to choose? The VNS analysts chose the gubernatorial election, in part because it had a slightly higher correlation with the exit poll data than the 1996 presidential election. But had they chosen the 1996 presidential election as the basis of comparison, the models would have shown a narrower gap between Gore and Bush at 7:45 on Election Night 2000, and it is likely that no one would have called Florida for Gore. (That type of problem was eliminated in 2004, because the new consortium operation expanded the models to give several estimates—based not on just one previous statewide contest, but on three previous contests.)

Talkov doesn't recollect that Gorman and Mishkin actually expressed reservations about Gore's lead, as Ellis later asserted, though if they did, they soon changed their minds. Fox called the race only three minutes after NBC and two minutes after CNN/CBS. What Talkov remembers is that the call was "routine . . . essentially a no-brainer," she told me in a 2005 interview. This was a sentiment echoed by Ellis in talking with his cousin, who phoned shortly after the networks made their announcements to ask if Ellis was sure. "Jeb, I'm sorry, I'm looking at a screenful of Gore."[8]

AT NINE O'CLOCK, when Mitofsky and Lenski had first seen the troubling numbers that suggested the Florida call for Gore may have been wrong, the decision team at Fox was busily scouring the computer screens for other state races. Ellis wrote in his post-election article that at some unspecified point, but apparently closer to ten than nine o'clock, he "checked the Florida data one more time, just to make sure Gore's key state was holding." He paged through the screens and found that they all indicated the race was too close to call. After the rest of the team examined the screens, the decision to rescind was unanimous. Ellis wrote that VNS had come to a similar decision and had already rescinded the call by the time Fox made its announcement.[9] But my notes show that it was Mitofsky and Lenski for CNN/CBS who first rescinded the call (at 9:54), followed shortly by ABC, and then Fox at 10:02. VNS and NBC, which first projected Gore the winner at 7:49, did not rescind until 10:15.[10]

As THE EVENING became morning, Talkov and the team projected winners in most of the other states. By 1:20 A.M., they were all focused on Florida as the key to the election. According to Ellis, they no longer needed the statistical models. He cited Mitofsky as claiming that at this time of the night/morning, it was "back-of-the-envelope stuff," a time when it was a matter of calculating by hand how the outstanding vote would break. In Ellis's words, "the game became 'need/get.'" How many votes did Gore "need" to close the gap, and what percentage of the votes was he projected to "get" in the precincts that had not yet reported?

Ellis wrote that at five minutes before two in the morning, he called George W. for a brief conversation and told the Texas governor that Gore could not win in Florida. A few minutes later, Ellis claimed, it became even clearer that Gore could not win, because the Democrat needed 64 percent of the outstanding vote to close the gap, but was getting just 60 percent. Still, the decision team hesitated, and it occurred to Ellis that all the other networks and AP were also reluctant to make the decisive call. No one wanted to be wrong twice in one evening. "That was fine with me," Ellis wrote. "We figured if Bush got to eight points of clearance on the need/get ratio, that would be more than comfortable."[11]

At a few minutes after two, he wrote, the crucial ratio occurred, and Ellis made the call—with no objection from any member of the decision team. At 2:16, Fox announced its call, and the other networks soon followed. AP and VNS did not make the call.

According to Talkov, when she read Ellis's account of the Bush call, "I freaked out. That was so far from what happened."[12] Ellis's claim that he based his projection on a statistical analysis, she said, "was a load of crap."[13]

If the wee hours of the morning was a time of "back-of-the-envelope" calculations, certainly Talkov, as Ellis's "statistical wizard," would have been part of that effort. But she was not doing any such calculations. Nor did she see any evidence that Ellis or Gorman or Mishkin was doing so either. Gorman and Mishkin were flipping through the screens and talking on the phones, while Ellis was spending most of his time also on the phone, to his cousins. If any of the men were calculating "need/get" ratios, they never shared those calculations with her, though every other call made by the team had first been passed by her for review. There was nothing the four of them were doing as a team that justified Ellis's statement that "*we* figured" Bush would win Florida once he got an eight-point clearance on the need/get ratio. As far as she could see, there was no "we," nor was there any "figuring."[14]

What Talkov remembers very clearly was that there was no group discussion of the outstanding vote, and that around two in the morning, Ellis was spending time on the phone with one or the other of his governor cousins. Perhaps, as he later wrote, he had in fact called them a little before two o'clock, but certainly not to announce the results of his statistical calculations. Perhaps, as he had also written, the purpose of his call was to obtain information from his cousins, especially from Jeb Bush, who according to Ellis was "wired into Florida."[15] In any case, whether he sought information or just got it gratis, the decision to call the race was triggered when Ellis excitedly announced, "Jebbie says we got it! Jebbie says we got it."

Gorman and Mishkin didn't object, perhaps because it was the Florida governor telling them that the vote count was decisive. Certainly, Ellis seemed convinced that Bush had won. Still, Talkov was uncomfortable with a call based not on the data in the models, but on the judgment of a partisan source, especially a source so close to one of the candidates. How could Jeb Bush know for certain? But then again he might. After all, he was the governor. And if anyone was "wired" into the vote count in that state, it had to be the governor.

Talkov feels sure that if she had objected to the call, Ellis would not have told Fox to announce it. Throughout the evening, her judgment had always been followed. And there had been no pressure from anyone at the Fox network about calling the races, either to call them faster, or to call them for anyone. The only pressure was the internal one from the four members of the team, knowing they were competing with the other networks. And all four of them wanted to be right. Even now, as Ellis was asking about his cousin's judgment that Bush had Florida, she felt certain that Ellis was himself convinced Jeb Bush was right—or Ellis wouldn't be suggesting they call it. "He was completely professional about that," she said.

In the end, she did not express an objection to the call, because if Ellis wanted to call the race based on outside information, rather than actual data, she figured that was his prerogative—given to him by the network. Later in the morning, as the race tightened and ultimately the call had to be rescinded, she felt angry with herself, and also embarrassed professionally, for not having objected when she had the chance. Then later, as it became clearer what had happened, she also became upset with the Bushes for having manipulated Ellis, and ultimately the Fox decision team, into making a call for George W. Bush—a call that she felt Jeb Bush must almost certainly have known was not justified, even as he sweet-talked his cousin into believing it was the right thing to do.

If Bush got to eight points of clearance on the
need/get ratio, that would be more than comfortable.
At the moment he did just that, we called Florida for Bush.

—*John Ellis, head of Fox decision team on Election Night 2000
and first cousin of George W. and Jeb Bush*

∎

The Fox projection had no impact on our decision
to call Florida for Bush.

—*Sheldon Gawiser, head of NBC election night projections*

∎

. . . this business about Fox pressuring other people to call,
I never made a projection in my life because of
some other network.

—*Warren Mitofsky, inventor of exit polls and original designer of network
consortium's election night projection system, co-director of CNN/CBS
decision team on Election Night 2000*

∎

Convictions are more dangerous foes of truth than lies.

—*Friedrich Nietzsche,* Human, All too Human

∎

5

The Bandwagon

One of the reasons the Ellis controversy didn't get more play is that none of the network decision teams would admit to being bamboozled by another network. Indeed, the general consensus among the press seemed to be that while it may have been questionable for Fox to have hired someone so close to the candidates to be in charge of calling the election, no real harm was done. After all, within four minutes of the Fox call, all the other networks made the same projection. And no network admitted doing so because of another network's actions. Thus, as Jack Shafer of the online magazine *Slate* wrote, "Although Ellis has been fairly upfront about rooting for his cousin, we need to remember that he was looking at the same data as Mitofsky and the other network seers who made the same call."[1] Conclusion: All the networks projected Bush the winner because of compelling data that demanded such a call, and it was just coincidence that Fox did it first.

Here is a very different scenario about what happened on Election Night 2000:

- The data provided by Voter News Service (VNS) on the computer screens did not make a compelling case for calling the election on behalf of George W. Bush. To the contrary, there was a compelling reason not to make the call.
- The Fox network called the election for Bush at 2:16 in the morning because Jeb Bush persuaded his cousin, John Ellis, to do so.
- Sheldon Gawiser at NBC called the election for Bush about a minute later, because Fox called the election first.
- Warren Mitofsky and Joe Lenski, co-directors of the joint CBS/CNN decision team, called the election for Bush immediately after NBC's call, because Fox and NBC had already called the election.
- ABC reluctantly called the election within four minutes of Fox, because at least one ABC executive, but not the decision team, felt pressured to avoid being the only network that still showed the presidential contest too close to call.

Lack of Compelling Data

One of the biggest myths surrounding the networks' miscall on Election Night 2000 is that about 2:10 in the morning, the VNS system provided overwhelming evidence that Bush was going to win Florida. It did not.

For several hours before the miscalls were made, exit poll results were no longer relevant. The system was reporting real vote counts in each of the counties in each of the states around the country. Those vote counts were being compiled by VNS. Once the votes were officially tallied in each precinct, a VNS representative would call in the results to have them entered into the VNS computers. Already entered into the computer were the vote totals in each county from previous elections. These vote histories allowed VNS to compare the number of votes already cast at any point during election night with the total number that would be "expected," given the history of voting in each county in each state. If typically a county had 10,000 votes in a presidential election, and the turnout in 2000 was assumed to be about the same as it was in the 1996 presidential election, the computer would know that if 6,000 votes had already been reported, about 4,000 more votes were still outstanding. It cannot be stressed too strongly that such estimates of the outstanding vote are often quite far off the actual total. That was certainly the case in 2000 in Florida.

There is another potential source of error in the late night/early morning projections. The vote count reported by the VNS representatives is not 100 percent accurate. Mistakes are made as the VNS representatives call in to report the vote tallies from the precincts. The sources of error are many, but the two most common are 1) the VNS representative either does not have, or does not report, accurate information for some reason, and 2) the computer programmer enters the wrong data into the computer. There were several such major errors in Florida alone on Election Night 2000.

These errors were not peculiar to 2000. In every election, the computer models predicting the outstanding vote are off to some degree, and the errors in the vote count are often significant as well. But as Murray Edelman told me in an interview in 2006, "The numbers take on a life of their own." People on the decision teams certainly know that such errors are possible, but when they get immersed in the computer projections they focus more on what the numbers are saying, rather than on the possibility that the figures are off from the true count by significant margins.[2]

This tendency to treat the numbers as though they are gospel worried Edelman as election 2000 approached. He had noticed that in the 1998 midterm elections, and again during the primaries in 2000, the network decision teams were projecting winners in close races much too quickly, treating the late-night/early-morning VNS numbers as though they were completely accurate. In the week before Election Night 2000, he sent a special memo to all of the decision teams,

reminding them that significant errors often occur during the data collection process.[3] He also sent a spreadsheet that showed in the 1996 and
the 1998 elections how far off the VNS estimates were from the official figures. In the past, the errors had amounted to more than one half
of one percent of the total vote count, he wrote, even when virtually all
of the votes had been counted in that state. The spread sheet showed,
specifically in Florida, that in the 1996 presidential election, VNS
estimated a total of 5,266,041 votes when the actual vote turned out to
be 5,303,794 votes—a VNS underestimation of almost 38,000 votes,
representing more than seven tenths of one percent of the total vote.[4]

At 2:16 in the morning following Election Night 2000, when Fox
projected Bush the Florida winner, the VNS system showed Gore
trailing Bush by just over 50,000 votes. Most of the estimated outstanding vote was in Democratic counties, so one could surmise that
Gore might be able to pick up at least 20,000 votes over Bush, and possibly even more, reducing the margin to about 30,000 votes or less.[5]
This margin was even smaller than the error Edelman had noted in the
spreadsheet. The race was clearly too close to call.

The situation demanded caution. The networks had already miscalled Florida for Gore early in the evening, although at that time a
Gore victory in Florida did not necessarily mean that he would win the
presidency. It was different at 2:15 in the morning. Everyone could see
that if Bush won Florida, he would get enough electoral votes to
become the next president. This was not a time for any decision team
to take chances. And if all the recipients of Edelman's memo and
spreadsheets had paid attention to his warning, no team would have
made the miscall.

The popular impression, however, is that *all* the decision teams miscalled Florida, because all of the networks projected Bush the winner
within four minutes of the Fox projection. In fact, among the six
decision teams—one each for Fox, NBC, CNN/CBS (which were
sharing one team), ABC, AP, and VNS—three of the teams projected
Bush the winner, and three refused to do so.

work I could ever imagine," and declared that Ellis "had no business talking to the Bush brothers or any other politician about what he was doing. Leaking results is common practice [even if illegal], but getting help from a politician does not make any sense. . . . That's the best way I know to get misled."[9]

On the other hand, Ellis's framing his contact with his cousins as "newsgathering" was adopted as a defense of Fox's decision team's behavior by Roger Ailes, chairman and CEO of Fox, during the congressional hearings held the following year.[10] Ailes, too, seemed to find nothing wrong with the possibility that Ellis could be asking Bush whether or not it was time to call the race for Bush.

IN HIS ACCOUNT of Election Night 2000, Ellis claims that he was calculating a "need/get" ratio to determine at what point Gore needed more votes than he could possibly get. The problem is that Ellis's description of how his need/get ratio changed over time does not accord with the official record. At five minutes before two in the morning, according to Ellis, he became convinced that Bush was going to win. He doesn't say what led to this epiphany, but if his conviction was at all influenced by actual data, rather than simply by the enthusiasm of his cousins, he should have become more optimistic about Bush's chances not at 1:55 A.M. but at 2:08 A.M., when an erroneous report from Volusia County caused a jump in Bush's lead of almost 20,000 votes. But Ellis seems unaware of this jump. He says that sometime after two, his need/get ratio was "roughly 64/60 and widening"—showing Gore needing 64 percent of the remaining votes but getting only 60 percent, a four-percentage-point deficit. The computer screen provided the percent of the estimated outstanding vote that Gore would need, but it did not provide a composite "get" figure. On the screens were listed all the counties with outstanding votes, and the percentage of votes going to Gore up until that time in each of the counties. There was no average "get" figure; each percentage figure applied to a specific county. Furthermore, the counties included numerous precincts, and that screen did not specify which precincts were not included in the count. If Gore had been getting 60 percent of the vote in the precincts that had already voted in a given county, that did not necessarily mean he would get 60 percent of the rest of the vote. His percentage could be higher or lower, depending on the types of precincts not yet included. If the predominantly black precincts in that county had not yet reported their vote, for example, Gore would get much more than the 60 percent he had been. But if the outstanding precincts were, say, dominated by voters with Cuban connections, Gore's estimated "get" figure would be lower.

Ellis asserts that at the moment his need/get ratio showed Gore trailing in his "get" figure by eight percentage points from what he would "need," Ellis called the race. The text makes clear that Ellis was describing a gradual "widening" of the gap from two o'clock on. But that is not what happened. Nowhere does he indicate any awareness that there was a sudden change in the vote totals at 2:08, a fact he could not help but notice if he really understood what was showing on the screens and if he were actually calculating a need/get ratio. Nor did he share any of his need/get calculations with the one person upon whom he had been relying the whole evening, his "statistical wizard," Cynthia Talkov, who sat right next to him for the thirteen hours of coverage. She never saw him make any of the "back-of-the-envelope" calculations he claimed to have made, and he never mentioned a need/get ratio to her or to the decision team more broadly as a basis for calling the election.

Another problem with Ellis's claim of a need/get calculation is that Ellis makes a big mistake in recounting what Gore's "need" figure actually was at the time of the Fox call. According to Ellis, "Gore's 'get' number remained constant at just under 60 percent. We were waiting for the lines to cross. Votes trickled in. Gore's 'need' seemed to increase with each new report."[11] Ellis does not tell the reader what the final need/get ratio was when he called the race, but he does say that there was a gap of eight percentage points. That would mean Gore's "need" figure was up to 68 percent, with his "get" figure remaining in the 60 percent level. In fact, at 2:16, when Fox projected Bush the winner, Gore's "need" figure shown on the VNS computer screen was at 63 percent, five percentage points below where it would have to be to fit Ellis's description.[12] Ellis is just plain wrong when he asserts that the need/get ratio, as he was supposedly calculating it, was sufficient (by Ellis's own standards) to make the call.

Apart from the inconsistency between Ellis's account of his supposed need/get calculations and the official record, there are several bizarre comments in his *Inside* article that suggest he had little understanding of the statistical nature of the data. He noted, for example, that Fox called New Hampshire—"as fine a call as I have ever seen; Gorman nailed it inside a razor-thin margin of error."[13] Perhaps Ellis was imagining a Red Sox game (he was a former columnist for the *Boston Globe*), with Gorman throwing a strike on the inside corner. But there is no way to "nail" a projection "inside a razor-thin margin of error." A margin of error is not thin or fat; it's simply a number. Moreover, if a candidate's lead is "within" a margin of error, it usually means the figure is too small to be statistically significant and would not justify a projection. That certainly was not the case when Fox made the call at 12:13 in the morning—seven minutes after VNS, and more than two hours after the other four networks. Why New Hampshire was such a "fine" call when Fox was dead last in making it is also a mystery. "Ellis makes the whole exercise sound like some wild west adventure," Mitofsky wrote in describing the *Inside* magazine article. "From what Ellis says he does not know how to read the screens. He is a knowledgeable political analyst, but it takes more than that to do the job. . . . I cannot, for the life of me, imagine what the hell Ellis is doing when he makes calls."[14]

It's not just the testimony of Talkov and Edelman and Mitofsky that calls into question Ellis's understanding of the election night projection system. The columnist's own words reveal a man who was in way over his head on Election Night 2000. However extensive his experience in reporting on elections, he was woefully ignorant of the arcane statistical measures that were part of the VNS system. Ellis's contention that he projected Bush the winner based on statistical calculations of VNS data defies credibility.

What really happened, of course, is that Ellis was not prompted to project Bush the winner in Florida by a mythical need/get ratio or by the data on the VNS computers screens. His need/get calculations, however inaccurate, could well have been made after the fact, as a cover for the real reason why Ellis made the call. What obviously got him excited about his cousin's chances in Florida was transmitted to the decision team members, when he excitedly announced, "Jebbie says we got it!" The Florida governor spoke, and Ellis acted.

NBC Follows Fox

At the moment that Fox announced to the world that Bush was the winner of Florida, VNS Editorial Director Murray Edelman was on the phone with Sheldon Gawiser, NBC's director of elections. Gawiser said he was thinking about calling Florida for Bush and wanted to know what Edelman thought.[15] Edelman was stunned. "Didn't you read my memo?" he asked, referring to the warning he had sent the previous week to the decision teams. But before Gawiser could respond, the Fox projection was announced on air, and according to Edelman, Gawiser terminated the phone conversation with the comment, "Gotta go. Fox just called it." A minute later, NBC projected Bush the winner in Florida.

Despite the close timing of the Fox and NBC calls, Gawiser says he did not call the race because of Fox. When I asked him in an interview in February 2006 why he had phoned Edelman before projecting Bush the winner,[16] he acknowledged that when he spoke with Edelman at 2:15 in the morning, he was not ready to call the race, though he was getting close to doing so. He asked Edelman if there was any-thing in the Florida data that would be a reason not to project Bush the winner. And, according to Gawiser, Edelman said no. I asked Gawiser if he recalled Edelman mentioning anything about the memo. Gawiser did not. I said that Edelman remembers specifically men-tioning the memo. "It was a very cryptic conversation," Gawiser said. "There was a lot of screaming and noise."

Did Gawiser call the race because Fox called it?

No, he said. He called the race because, as he was talking with Edel-man, he was also monitoring the computer screens and saw a spike in the VNS data. And that's what prompted him to cut off the phone con-versation and call the race.

Sitting next to Edelman when he got the call from Gawiser was Clyde Tucker, a statistician who had worked with the projection sys-tem on many election nights, and who is currently the decision team leader for CNN. In an interview in 2005[17], he said he definitely remembers that Edelman mentioned the memo to Gawiser, but that the conversation was short and Edelman didn't have time to elaborate before the NBC decision team leader ended the conversation. Edelman remembered, too, that the conversation was short-lived. When he got the call, he had been focusing on another part of the election, and was taken aback when Gawiser suggested calling Florida. By the time he recovered and tried to talk about the memo, Gawiser was no longer listening.

Trevor Tompson, currently manager of news surveys for the Asso-ciated Press, told me he was sitting next to Edelman and Tucker dur-ing Election Night 2000. He doesn't recall specifically the call from Gawiser, but he does recall that Edelman mentioned his memo several times on the phone early in the morning when calls came in asking about calling Florida for Bush. "Murray was puzzled why anyone would call it," Tompson said. "He was telling everyone about his memo."[18]

Lenski and Mitofsky wrote in their post-election "timeline" report that Edelman had talked with them after the election about Gawiser's call at 2:15 in the morning. "Murray told us that he told Shelly that he would not make a call of that magnitude at that time but that he could provide no argument against NBC making the call."[19] Edelman adamantly denies he ever made such a statement to Lenski and Mitofsky. Clearly, there is some misunderstanding among these colleagues.

Despite the contradictions on some points, no one disputes that Edelman made it clear to everyone, including Gawiser, that he would not project Bush the winner in Florida because of the importance of the call, especially given the miscall earlier in the evening. The dispute comes over whether Edelman tried to remind Gawiser about errors in the data, as pointed out previously in Edelman's memo, and whether Edelman said he could give Gawiser no reason why NBC should not call the race. I think it's possible that Gawiser had in fact asked Edelman whether there was something in the data that meant Florida shouldn't be called, and in the confusion of the moment, Edelman might well have said no. After all, that was the truth. If one believed the data to be completely accurate, there was no reason not to call the race. Edelman's concern was always with the quality of the data, and he did indicate to Gawiser, as the NBC team leader acknowledges, that Edelman did not recommend making the call. But Edelman had no time to explain why a call was not warranted, because Gawiser cut the connection as soon as Fox made the call.

Both Edelman and Gawiser agree the conversation was "cryptic" and short, leaving no time for Edelman to elaborate on the reasons why he was against the projection. Had Fox not made the call, the conversation could have proceeded, and Edelman would have had time to remind Gawiser of the potential errors that could occur, as outlined in the memo and in the spreadsheets. Unbeknownst to both of them, just four minutes earlier, the AP vote count showed a sudden drop in Bush's lead to less than 48,000 votes. Now, at the very moment that Fox called the race, the AP lead for Bush fell another 17,000 votes,[20] a drop that would have stopped any network (except perhaps Fox) from projecting Bush the winner. Had Edelman been able to delay NBC's call by just a few minutes, the AP information may well have been shared with the other network decision teams, thus precluding their miscalls.

Gawiser maintains that he terminated the conversation with Edelman not because of Fox, but because of that spike in the VNS data. But the VNS data showing a sharp increase in Bush's lead came at 2:08 in the morning, not between 2:15 and 2:16, and was no doubt the reason Gawiser phoned Edelman in the first place. For Gawiser to say now that it was not Fox's call, but the change in VNS data, which led to the NBC projection is to confuse the two events. "I believe those two things were simultaneous," he said.[21] But they were not. They happened eight minutes apart.

Edelman is convinced that if the Fox projection had not been announced at that moment, he could have persuaded Gawiser to hold off on making the call for NBC. In the past, Edelman said, Gawiser had consulted with him about close calls, and would probably have held back as long as everyone else did—especially if Edelman had been able to remind the NBC decision team leader of the potential data errors. But Edelman never got to do that. When Fox called Florida, Gawiser bolted.

CNN/CBS: "Me, too!"

In their post-election report to CBS and CNN,[22] Mitofsky and Lenski write, "We can honestly say that we did not feel any pressure to call the Florida race prematurely." They point out that they resisted pressure on other races throughout the evening, not calling the fourth electoral vote in Maine for several hours after others had projected the winner there, and refusing to call the presidential race in Alabama for twenty-five minutes after VNS projected Bush the winner in that state, until they felt assured the call would hold. They also delayed calling the U.S. Senate race in Montana, because a Republican victory there gave the GOP control of the U.S. Senate, and again they wanted to be sure before making such a significant call. "This being said," they write, "we think it would not have been possible to hold out on a call for a Bush presidency when the data at that time gave us no reason to argue against the call. The only argument against calling Bush the winner in Florida at 2:17 A.M. would have been considering the errors that we have seen in Florida throughout the night 'we don't trust the VNS vote count.' As it turns out that would have been the correct answer, but we had no way of knowing that at that time."

Actually, they did have a way of knowing the correct answer. In fact, they already knew it. Mitofsky himself had warned me of the problem with data errors only an hour earlier, about 1:07, after I asked him why he didn't call the race in Florida if he was so certain Bush would win. His reply (worth reprinting in this context): "Do you want to call the president of the United States on the basis of 30,000 votes? Right now Bush leads by 65,000 votes and at three in the morning he'll likely have a 30,000-vote margin. Are you comfortable with that? I'm not. Vote counts are not one hundred percent sure. Some end-of-night vote counts are off by at least one point . . . the counts are reported by the media . . . and they make mistakes."

According to Lenski and Mitofsky, Bush's lead just before they projected him the winner in Florida at 2:17 was a mere 51,433 votes, with an estimated 97 percent of the precincts counted. The two pollsters estimated that Gore would probably not be able to reduce that margin by more than about 20,000 votes (although ultimately it was about 25,000 votes, which shows how shaky such estimates can be), leaving Bush's margin at 31,433 votes. This was exactly the same situation that Mitofsky had warned me about only an hour earlier. As he said, "Some end-of-night vote counts are off by at least one point"— or, in this case, 60,000 votes. So, how could he possibly justify a projection with a margin only half that size?

The difference between 1:07, when Mitofsky warned me about possible errors in the data, and 2:17, when he and Lenski essentially ignored their own cautionary instincts and called the race for Bush, was that two networks had already made the call. Neither of the two pollsters likes to think they were pressured by those calls, and in their post-election report they describe a series of events that conforms with a non-pressured, rational decision-making process. They note that Fox called the race at 2:16, and that "our immediate reaction was frustration because we were within minutes of calling the race ourselves. We spent the next ninety seconds confirming our numbers." At 2:17 they note that NBC called Florida. A minute later they note, "We concluded our review of the data and advised CBS and CNN to call Florida and the Presidency for Bush."

The official CBS review, with information provided by the decision team leaders, reinforces this very calm approach to making the Florida call. "The team was preparing to make the call when it heard Fox declare Florida for Bush, and the CBS News Decision Team thought, 'Darn, we're going to be second.' Then NBC called Florida for Bush and the team said, 'Well, third.' The people on the CBS News Decision Desk took another 30 seconds to finish their data check."[23]

But that's not exactly what happened. After Fox called Florida for Bush, the team may well have thought "Darn, we're going to be second," but Mitofsky said, "Fox has an agenda, don't forget!" And according to my notes written at the time—when I had no inclination as to the significance of the details, but was just writing what happened—it was just a minute later, at 2:17 in the morning, when a voice in the CBS/CNN decision room announced, "NBC called Florida for Bush." I didn't hear Mitofsky or Lenski say, "Well, third," though they may well have been thinking that. I did hear Mitofsky respond immediately, "We'll call it, too!" The official record of calls, as produced by CBS, confirms my record of a more immediate response. Unlike the CBS report, which says the decision team "took another 30 seconds to finish their data check" before deciding to call the race, the record shows that NBC made the call at 2:17:30, and CBS did so at 2:17:52, just twenty-two seconds later. That twenty-two-second lag time was the time that it took for Mitofsky's immediate decision following the NBC call to be conveyed from the decision desk to Kathleen Frankovic at CBS, to the producers, and then to Dan Rather. It was not used by Mitofsky and Lenski to calmly review the data and then decide that Bush was the inevitable winner.

There is more than a subtle difference between their post-election account of a calm, unpressured review of the data for another thirty seconds to a minute, and my own notes showing an immediate decision after NBC announced its projection of the winner in Florida. The latter suggests that indeed the two pollsters were influenced by the calls of the other two networks, and they wanted to make sure they were not left behind as the Bush train roared its way out of the station. Their admitted initial reaction of "frustration," that a network had called it before them, shows that there was an internal competitive pressure. They weren't able to call the race first, but they surely did not want to be last. And in the process, they forgot all about the potential errors in the data.

Mitofsky strongly disagrees that his call after the NBC announcement was prompted by the Fox and NBC calls. He says when he gave me the warning at 1:07 in the morning about not calling the presidency on the basis of 30,000 voters, "far fewer votes had been counted than were counted at 2:16. That margin looked more imposing with 97 percent of the precincts supposedly counted [as erroneously reported by the VNS screens] than it did when we first talked."[24] But this argument doesn't address his warning at 1:07—which was that after *all* the votes have been counted, not just 97 percent but 100 percent, error in the vote count could be as much as one percent of the total vote. That would mean as much as 60,000 votes. Even at 2:16 in the morning, with 97 percent of the vote supposedly counted, the projected margin of victory was much smaller than the possible error—meaning that adherence to Mitofsky's warning would have dictated no projection be made.

Mitofsky also disputes that his call was triggered by Fox and NBC, because "at the time Fox made its call Joe and I were systematically going through the county file looking for unusual numbers in any county. We did not have the tools then to spot anomalies like what happened in Volusia. Nonetheless, we were looking at each county one at a time to see if anything struck us. That was the last step before making the call. We had already alerted the control room about what we were considering *before* Fox made its call."[25]

My notes at the time can neither confirm nor deny Mitofsky's recollection that he and Lenski had already alerted the control room about their review. Even had they done so, the review did not necessarily mean they would have made the call. It's in retrospect that they seem to forget about the error in the vote count, something that was clearly on Mitofsky's mind at one in the morning, and almost certainly, I believe, would have been on his mind at 2:15—if no other network had made a call.

Perhaps recognizing that their explanation for the 2:17 call may not be persuasive to everyone, they argue "with the data that we were provided with at 2:40 A.M. we would have most certainly made the call then if we had not already made the call at 2:17 A.M.. We would not have been doing our jobs if we had declined to project the race based upon such convincing data." Again, that assumes the "convincing data" were correct.

They further justify that view by noting that according to news reports, the Gore campaign had been looking at the same numbers as had the decision team, and had come to the same conclusion that their candidate had lost. "It is unlikely," they write, "that the Gore campaign made this decision solely based upon the network projections. Their own independent reading of the vote data at that time, according to the news stories, showed that they had no chance of pulling off the win."[26]

Here the two pollsters are just plain misinformed, and they underestimate the power of the news media. As indicated in chapter 1 of this book, Jeffrey Toobin reported that Gore telephoned Bush to concede solely on the basis of the network projection at 2:20 in the morning, not on the basis of vote-count data at 2:30 or 2:40, nor because the Gore campaign's own independent data analysis confirmed the expected defeat. In fact, Gore's own operatives were appalled that Gore was going to concede.[27]

Mitofsky's and Lenski's claim that they would have called the race at 2:40 if they hadn't already done so by 2:17 is not persuasive. The situation as shown by the VNS data was only slightly better for Bush at 2:40 than it was twenty-three minutes earlier, with his projected winning margin now up to about 40,000 instead of 30,000 votes — still a figure that was too small to be trusted. A more plausible scenario if neither Fox nor NBC had called the race is that the AP data, showing a sudden drop in Bush's lead at 2:16 in the morning, and then another sudden drop six minutes later to just 15,000 votes, would have been brought to the networks' attention. Indeed, AP's David Pace indicates that by 2:30 in the morning, he almost certainly would have alerted the networks to the discrepancy in the figures between VNS and AP, thus preventing a call by any of the networks.[28]

It's also possible that Lenski and Mitofsky would have made a more aggressive effort to find out what other sources of the vote count were showing. They are correct in saying that the VNS data errors from Volusia County at 2:08 were not corrected until 2:48. But VNS wasn't the only source of vote counts. It wasn't until after three in the morning, when one of their staff members noted a decline in Bush's lead, that the decision team leaders acknowledge "we *began* tracking numbers on the Florida secretary of state's web site and the AP."[29] But if they had not yet called the race, nor had anyone else, they almost certainly would have begun checking to see what AP was showing much earlier than three in the morning.

The contrast between the cautious Mitofsky a little after one in the morning and the more aggressive Mitofsky an hour and ten minutes later is that in the interim he had succumbed to the temptation that Edelman described—allowing the numbers to "take on a life of their own." Even at 2:15, just before Fox announced that Bush had won,

Mitofsky said to me, *"If the numbers are correct,* Bush will win Florida." But after the two networks announced their calls, the cautionary clause got lost . . . and it was "Bush will win Florida." At that point, Mitofsky was focused more on what the numbers seemed to be saying and less on the real and dangerous possibility that they were just plain wrong.

EDELMAN NOTES THAT many people misunderstand the psychological dynamics of calling a close race, that in fact the dynamics are much different when a decision team is the first to call a race from when a team is making the call after others have already done so. To be the first to call a close race, especially one like the Florida call with all of its implications, is quite risky, and decision teams naturally hold back— looking for reasons why they should *not* call it and possibly embarrass themselves and their networks. That is why it is quite likely that had Fox and NBC not made the Florida call, Lenski and Mitofsky would have sought out other sources of the vote count, to see if those sources agreed with VNS or provided a different picture. That's also why Gawiser called Edelman, to see if there was a reason *not* to make a call that the data seemed to support.

Once one network has made a projection, however, the dynamics work in exactly the opposite direction. Instead of finding reasons not to call the race, the rest of the decision teams are looking for reasons to go along with the other networks that have made the calls. The very fact that another team has made a call can by itself be sufficient reason, because it means that other experts obviously agree that the data support the call. But if a team still has doubts, as did Mitofsky and Lenski about the first call ("Fox has an agenda, don't forget"), their review of the numbers will inevitably be biased in favor of finding support. In this case a quick review of just the VNS data revealed no contradictory evidence, and thus they saw no reason to look further by going to the AP or the Florida secretary of state's Web site. And, of course, the NBC call following the one by Fox provided the confirmation that prompted Mitofsky to jump on the bandwagon and say, "We'll call it, too!" Lost in the excitement of the moment was the caution that the numbers may not be correct.

The ultimately impossible task faced by Edelman was to prevent the very first call. He had a fighting chance to do that, because Gawiser had telephoned, asking to be persuaded not to make the projection. But all was lost once Ellis announced, "Jebbie says we got it!"

ABC Succumbs Twice to Network Pressure

That ABC called the Florida election for Gore at 8:02 on election night and then for Bush at 2:20 the next morning is a testament to the force of pack journalism. For both calls, the ABC election projection experts said no. But ABC executives overrode their experts in an ironical and vain attempt not to look foolish.

There was a reason ABC was the last member of the consortium to project Gore the winner in Florida in the early evening of Election Day. The network had hired two special statistical consultants to examine why VNS had erroneously called the wrong winner in the U.S. Senate race in New Hampshire four years earlier. They discovered a decidedly Democratic bias in the exit polls, and had devised a rule of thumb to prevent ABC from going along with another VNS mistake in 2000. When these experts were asked whether to project Gore the winner in Florida along with the other networks, with VNS indicating more than a 99 percent chance the vice president would win, one of the experts said he saw it more as an 85 percent chance. And both experts opposed making the call. "It wasn't like we were calling an off-year dogcatcher race in North Dakota," said one of those consultants, Kenneth Goldstein. "Besides, what's the hurry?" But, as Alicia Shepherd wrote in the *American Journalism Review*, "Despite the misgivings of its experts, ABC's team couldn't resist the competitive pressure, and ABC decision desk chief Carolyn Smith made the call."[30]

A similar situation faced the network six hours later, again with all the other networks already projecting Bush the winner in Florida and the ABC experts firmly opposed. Smith asked John Blydenburgh, a long-time consultant to ABC, what he thought, after the other networks had called the race. "I told her I wouldn't touch it!" he told me in an interview in January 2006. "The data had been wrong all night long. You couldn't trust it." He said the VNS fieldwork was shoddy, the quality control poor, the selection of sample precincts erroneous, and the data tabulation of the numbers once they were entered into the system problematic. The recommendation of the decision team was also against a call. "I know she agreed with me," Blydenburgh said of Carolyn Smith. He is convinced that if all the networks had not called Florida, ABC certainly would not have either. "But somebody [at ABC] called it anyway," Blydenburgh said. "I don't know who. I wasn't on the telephone call." He added, "Carolyn took the fall for ABC, but she will never admit it. She's too loyal."[31] Whoever authorized the call, ABC projected Bush the next president of the United States at 2:20 in the morning, the last network to do so.

AP Resists the Pressure

At almost precisely the moment Jeb Bush told his cousin "We got it!", the AP vote count showed the Bush margin narrowing to just over 30,000 votes. That drop was part of a longer decline which, according to AP figures, showed a Bush lead of about 64,000 votes at 1:42, dropping to 56,000 at 1:52, to under 48,000 at 2:12 and then plummeting by more than 17,000 votes four minutes later. By 2:30, after all the networks had announced Bush as the next president of the United States, AP still had not called Florida. "Across the country, newspapers were bumping up against their final deadlines," Shepherd wrote. "Editors were edgy. Dozens of the AP's 1,500 daily newspaper members began calling New York, Washington, Miami. Why hasn't the AP called the race?"[32] Bush's lead was down now to 19,000 votes.

At the time of the networks' calls, the AP decision team leader on Election Night 2000, David Pace,[33] was also unaware of the declining Bush margin in the AP data. Numerous reports after the election explained AP's refusal to call Florida for Bush by noting that the AP had its own source of data. But those reports were wrong. Pace says he wasn't looking at AP data, but at the same VNS data as were the other network decision team leaders, including Gawiser, and Mitofsky and Lensik. And Pace saw no reason to call Florida. "It was getting close," he said, "but because of the reversal [the earlier miscall and rescission in Florida], we were even more cautious than usual. There's no education like the second kick of a mule."

Pace was shocked when the networks projected Bush the winner. "I immediately called Murray to see what he was thinking," he said. "He reminded me of his memo and the spreadsheets—the difference [between the VNS count and the final vote count] in some states of one to two to three percent."

Pace relayed the information to Kevin Walsh, the AP Florida bureau chief, who told Pace what AP's numbers showed. "We were getting hammered by the papers," Pace said. "It was past deadline and they wanted to know why we hadn't called it." At 2:30, the president and CEO of AP, Louis D. Boccardi, called the Washington, D.C., decision team with the same question as the newspaper editors. The decision team called in Will Lester, AP's poll writer, with more than a decade of experience covering elections in Florida to get his opinion. After looking at the data, he said, "You can't do it."[34]

At 2:37, after its analysts concluded that Gore could still close the gap with late votes from Broward and Palm Beach counties, AP issued an urgent warning that despite the networks' call, there was "the narrowest of margins" between Bush and Gore, with many votes yet to be counted. "By that time newspaper Web sites were printing 'Bush Wins'," said AP Executive Editor Jonathan Wolman. "Gore had conceded to Bush. There was doom and gloom in Nashville. We felt extremely lonely. We were thinking, 'Florida's the whole ball game. Don't blow it.'"[35]

A little over an hour later, the wire service was vindicated, as all of the networks rescinded their calls, and the battle for the presidency began again.

IN THE 2006 interview, Pace said had the networks not called Florida by 2:20 in the morning, he might well have contemplated calling the race by 2:30 or so. At that point he would have consulted with both the Washington and Florida bureau chiefs—their decision making "was very much a consultative process"—and would have discovered the discrepancy between the AP and VNS vote counts. "I would immediately have told Murray," he said, and Edelman would have alerted the networks' decision teams right away. Pace said he actually did warn Edelman of a VNS/AP vote discrepancy at about three in the morning. By then, all the networks had called New Mexico for Gore, but AP had not yet made the call, nor had VNS. When Pace thought about projecting Gore the winner there, he first spoke with the AP bureau chief in that area, who cautioned against making the call because of vote problems in Bernalillo County. Immediately, Pace called Edelman. "Thanks," Edelman said. "But it's too late. I just called it."

Still, the fact that Pace and Edelman consulted with each other so often suggests that if only the networks had waited a few more minutes to call Florida for Bush, they might well have not made the call at all. In the meantime, it was likely Pace would have seen the discrepancy between the AP and VNS vote totals in Florida, and shared them with the networks—thus preventing the erroneous calls. It's also possible that Gawiser, and Mitofsky and Lenski, would have begun looking earlier at the AP and Florida websites for what these other vote counters were showing. The Florida call for Bush was not inevitable, even given the faulty VNS data. Without Jeb Bush's intervention, the networks might very well have portrayed the election results for what they really were early in the morning after Election Day—too close to call.

VNS has a long and enviable track record of accuracy in projecting races over the years. In the November election, however, VNS fell short.

—*Statement of ABC News Concerning the 2000 Election Projection, January. 2001*

The unique circumstances of the Florida election exposed problems at VNS that must now be corrected.

—*Andrew Heyward, president, CBS News, February 14, 2001*

If VNS is not reformed, we will pull out and will support a potential successor organization should VNS fail to meet CNN's requirements.

—*Tom Johnson, chairman and CEO, CNN*

In hindsight we made a significant error in relying on VNS data alone, although that was the only data available.

—*Roger Ailes, chairman and CEO, Fox News Network*

VNS has to be retooled or replaced. . . . The data our experts relied upon on election night was flawed in a number of ways.

—*Andrew Lack, president, NBC News*

When the Bush call was made . . . the data didn't support the call. . . . And VNS did not make the Bush call, the networks did.

—*Paul Biemer, statistical consultant, Research Triangle Institute, after evaluating the VNS system*

6

Scapegoat

In the immediate aftermath of the 2000 election night fiasco, with the legal and political fight between Gore and Bush still under way, House Republicans opened a separate front with an attack on the networks for biased coverage. Their claim was that networks delayed calling victories in states where Bush had sizeable leads, but at the same time quickly projected the winner in states where Gore had comparable leads. On November 15, congressman Billy Tauzin (R-Louisiana), then chair of the House Commerce Subcommittee on Telecommunications, Trade and Consumer Protection, charged that congressional investigators had found network delays in calling nine states that Bush won by at least six percentage points, but no delays in any state that Gore won by the same margin.[1] "By calling the Al Gore states early and delaying the calls on the George W. Bush states you receive a picture of America believing that Al Gore was sweeping the country and George W. Bush was having trouble carrying his states," said Tauzin. He added that the information painted "a very disturbing picture, I think, of probable bias."[2] The theory here was that this falsely positive news for Gore discouraged Bush voters in more western parts of the country from turning out to vote for the GOP candidate, a deliberate intention of the television networks.

Separate allegations were made by other Republicans, such as Representative Cliff Stearns (R-Florida), who claimed that thousands of potential Bush votes were lost when most of the networks projected Gore the winner in Florida shortly before eight in the evening. At that time, the polls were still open in the state's panhandle, where the closing time is an hour later than it is for the rest of the state.[3] Stearns's charge was picked up by the conservative organization Accuracy in Media (AIM), which had also acknowledged the damage done to Gore by the networks' premature call for Bush in Florida. AIM suggested that up to 10,000 voters had been discouraged from voting in the Florida panhandle because of the early erroneous call for Gore. Tauzin vowed to hold investigative hearings into the timing of network calls either in December or after the new Congress took office in January.

The charges of deliberate network bias were hardly credible, and seemed at best a smokescreen at the time to create a more negative political environment for Gore as he tried to obtain a hand recount in Florida. Fox has never been accused of having a liberal bias, yet the timing of that network's calls during Election Night 2000 was not remarkably different from that of other networks. Moreover, to the extent there was a problem with the networks' projections of winners, it was that the networks were too competitive with each other, not that they were laying back to favor either candidate. Representative Edward Markey (D-Massachusetts) got to the heart of the pretense that the "early calls were part of a vast left-wing conspiracy" when he asked caustically whether "dozens of network journalists, the staff of the Voter News Service, all of the network news directors, a score of election night anchors, and the President's first cousin [were] all co-conspirators in an intricately designed plot to call key states early for Vice President Gore?"[4]

The second charge, that thousands of Bush voters were discouraged from voting in Florida's panhandle because of the early Gore projection, seemed to die a natural death from sheer lack of plausibility. In 1985, after projecting winners in several states during the 1984 presidential election where the polls had not closed, all the networks promised to refrain from such calls in the future until "most" of the polling precincts had closed. In 2000, when NBC, CBS, CNN, and Fox projected Gore the winner in Florida several minutes before eight, most of the polls in the state were in fact closed. But because Florida's panhandle is on Central Time, the polls there were scheduled to remain open another eight to ten minutes after the Gore projection. That situation led to the wild speculation about the thousands of Bush voters discouraged from voting because the presidential election was already decided. But the truth is that any residents who expected to vote by the seven o'clock deadline, local time, would already have been in line or in the car or on foot headed toward their precinct's voting location. The notion that somehow 10,000 voters, only minutes away from casting their ballots, learned about the network projection and then decided it was no longer worthwhile to vote seems rather fanciful at best. And no credible evidence was offered to substantiate the charge.[5]

By the time of the hearings, on February 14, 2001, with Bush safely in the White House, Tauzin had dropped any claim of deliberate network bias in the election night coverage. In his opening statement, he announced that while there appeared to be a statistical bias in the VNS models that tended to favor Democrats, "The good news is that we discovered no evidence of intentional bias, no evidence of intentional slanting of this information."[6]

THOUGH THE MAJOR purpose of the hearing had been eliminated, with Tauzin's admission that his charges of bias were not valid, the Republican congressman proceeded to schedule testimony from the network chiefs anyway. The goal now, according to one reporter, was to "flog them publicly for making early projections that led the nation astray."[7] Adding insult to injury, the committee forced them to sit in the audience and listen to five hours of testimony before they would be called to give their own views. So churlish was this tactic that one of the new committee members, Rep. Steve Buyer (R-Indiana), chastised Tauzin: "If this is the culture of the Energy and Commerce Committee . . . it's one I find distasteful."[8]

For their part, the network executives also found the whole hearing distasteful. It was billed not as a fact-finding hearing, to gather information for new legislation that could possibly benefit the voter, but an "investigative" hearing, the type that is conducted when there is potential malfeasance or criminal activity. As such the event raised serious issues related to freedom of the press. Tauzin appeared to be in a fix, not wanting to be seen as backing down from his previous reckless statements, but perhaps also not wanting to be seen as violating the press's First Amendment rights, which at least by the standards of most reasonable people would be considered an inauspicious start for someone who had just been elevated to chairman of the Commerce Committee. Regardless of whether Tauzin entertained such concerns, he seemed to bend over backward to reassure the network chiefs that the committee only wanted to hear what the networks had to say, "recognizing the very sensitive First Amendment rights of the reporters and the networks to report the news as they see fit, recognizing that we would defend your right to do it wrong if you really wanted to."[9] This was a far different tone from the one Tauzin had used when it was still unclear who would win the presidency.

Still, this new attitude did not deter Roger Ailes, chairman and chief executive officer of Fox News Network, from voicing his concern: "I am deeply disappointed that this is being handled as an investigative and not a legislative, fact finding matter," he said. "I am further disappointed that this committee views its role as adversarial, requiring us to take an oath as if we have something to hide. We do not."[10]

His comments were echoed by Louis D. Boccardi, president and CEO of the Associated Press: "We believe that such an official government inquiry into essentially editorial matters, summoning the people who sit here, is inconsistent with the First Amendment values that are fundamental to our society," he said. "We agree that there were serious shortcomings, call them terrible mistakes—I do, in the election reporting of November 7 and 8—and that these mistakes cannot be allowed to happen again. But fixing them is a job for the nation's editors, not its legislators."[11]

And they had a lot of fixing to do. Or at least, VNS had a lot of fixing to do. According to the testimony of each network chief, the main problems with calling the wrong races on election night were caused by incorrect data from VNS. They did admit that there were "competitive pressures" among the networks, and that competition won out over accuracy. In the future, that competition could be better contained by insulating the decision desks from knowledge about projections made by the other networks. ABC and NBC promised to take this route; the other networks did not.

Despite pointing to competition as a major problem, oddly enough no network chief admitted that competitive pressures actually caused any wrong call. The two most important miscalls were the ones for Florida—Gore at about eight in the evening, and Bush at a quarter after two in the morning. But all of the network chiefs, briefed of course by their decision teams, blamed the two miscalls on bad VNS data, not on the decision teams who jumped the gun.

The testimony of David Westin, president of ABC News, is a case in point. He explained why his network would henceforth isolate its decision team so that it would not know what calls the other networks were making. "We could have served our viewers better if we had insulated them [the professional analysts] better from the competitive pressures that inevitably arise," he testified at the hearing. "I can tell you that if you sit there and four of your competitors have projected the next President of the United States and you haven't, there is a lot of competitive pressure, no matter what anybody tells you."[12]

If this is the solution, then it's logical to conclude that part of the problem on Election Night 2000 was that the ABC decision team actually succumbed to competitive pressures. That's what ABC's long-time consultant, John Blydenburgh, says was the case. But that's not what Westin was willing to admit. An article in the *American Journalism Review* had already revealed that ABC had ignored its own, specially hired statistical consultants, who had recommended against both Florida calls.[13] At the hearing, no one asked Westin why his network overrode the experts, but in a follow-up letter, the ranking Democrat, Rep. John D. Dingell of Michigan, referenced the article and then asked the ABC president that hard question. "Your experts stated that they did not believe the first Florida call should have been made because of the limited exit poll data and the lack of knowledge about absentee voting" Dingell wrote. "They did not believe the second Florida call should have been made because the absentee vote was not all in, and that there could be errors in the vote tallies. But these experts were overridden by the journalist running your decision desk. Please explain why." Clearly, this was the time for Westin to 'fess up to the influence of competitive pressures. Instead, he stonewalled.

Dingell did not know, of course, that the "journalist running the decision desk" had in fact opposed making the second call, and Westin did nothing to correct the record. "While we will not comment on the precise deliberations of the journalists who staffed the desk on election night," he wrote, "the decision team assigned to make the Florida projection took all available information into account. As shown on the decision screens made available to the committee, the data and the statistical models fully supported the projection of ABC News for Vice President Gore in Florida at the time it was made."[14] Note that he doesn't say what recommendation the decision team actually made, just that it "took all available information into account," leaving the impression that the decision team supported calling the race for Gore. Then he jumps to the statement that the statistical models supported a Gore projection, which is correct, but it does not address the skepticism that his specially hired statistical experts expressed about the validity of the models, and thus their recommendation not to make the call. Instead, he leaves the impression that competition played no role in the decision, that the projection was fully justified by the erroneous VNS data. The record shows, however, that ABC made the call only after the other four networks had done so, putting ABC in exactly the situation that Westin admitted creates "a lot of competitive pressure, no matter what anybody tells you." Including himself.

In the rest of his written response, Westin simply ignored the second part of Dingell's question—why ABC made the projection for Bush the following morning, when again his experts recommended against it. After addressing the Gore projection, Westin's written answer just stopped. No mention at all of the network's Florida call for Bush. It is a glaring omission to anyone who carefully reads Dingell's letter and Westin's response. Since Westin's letter was a specially prepared written document two months after the hearings, the failure to address the Bush projection could not have been an oversight. No doubt Westin did not want to enter anything into the record that was false. Nor did he want to admit that it wasn't VNS's fault that ABC made the Bush projection, but rather the fault of a network executive who made the decision. The very carefully constructed response avoids making a false statement, even as it gives the wrong impression about what really happened. If the truth had been known, Dingell could have asked the obvious—how insulating the decision desk from knowledge of what the other networks are doing would solve the problem of Election Night 2000, if an executive who has the authority to override the decision team is left free to roam the building.

Perhaps the testimony most notable for its sheer cheek came from Fox's Roger Ailes. In his prepared statement, he said that he had personally known John Ellis for over twenty years and that "he is a consummate professional." He noted that "much ado" had been made about a column Ellis wrote in 1999 for the *Boston Globe*, "where he stated in effect that his loyalty to then Governor George W. Bush would prevent him from writing further columns about politics." Despite noting Ellis's admitted conflict of interest, Ailes found no fault with it, but seemed proud to declare "we at Fox News do not discriminate against people because of their family connections." He admitted he was aware that John Ellis was speaking to Jeb and George W. Bush on election night. "Obviously, through his family connections, Mr. Ellis has very good sources," he wrote. "I do not see this as a fault or shortcoming of Mr. Ellis. Quite the contrary, I see this as a good journalist talking to his very high level sources on election night. By the way, Mr. Gorman and Mr. Mishkin were speaking to high level Democratic sources throughout the evening."[15]

There it was—the "news-gathering" excuse that Ellis had offered in his *Inside* article two months earlier to excuse a glaring conflict of interest—now being parroted by the Fox News chief. Not only that, two other team members had also engaged in conflict-of-interest behavior, providing a bipartisan cast that apparently in Ailes's mind gave it additional legitimacy. It's difficult to find a clearer example of conflict of interest than allowing Bush's cousin to confer with Bush about when to call the election for Bush. Ailes's refusal to acknowledge anything wrong with that behavior, and instead to praise it, reflects a rather unusual view of professional ethics.

The internal review that Fox undertook after the election included an interview with Cynthia Talkov, Ellis's "statistical wizard." The Fox attorney asked her if she could remember anything that Ellis had said to his cousins, any proprietary information that he might have given. Talkov said she had not listened closely to Ellis' personal conversations, and could not confirm that he had given them such information. During the interview, she also related to the Fox attorney why Ellis had suggested calling Florida for Bush, that Ellis had called the race after announcing "Jebbie says we got it." Inga Parsons, Talkov's attorney who was part of the phone conversation, has a "vivid recollection of a pregnant pause," as though the information about Ellis's call had stunned the Fox attorney into silence. Fox executives were interested in whether Ellis had violated the VNS contract by sharing information with the Bushes. The notion that the information might have gone in the other direction may not have been on their radar screen. After a few moments the conversation resumed, but the Fox attorney did not pursue the matter.[16]

At the hearing, Ailes stressed that Fox's internal investigation of Election Night 2000 had "found not one shred of evidence that Mr. Ellis revealed information to either or both of the Bush brothers which he should not have, or that he acted improperly or broke any rules or policies of either Fox News or VNS."[17] No reference was made about the real conflict of interest, which allowed one Bush brother essentially to project the other brother as the Florida winner.

Even on the issue of illegally sharing information with the Bush brothers, it's difficult to take Ailes seriously when he claims to have found "not one shred of evidence" for such actions. How much of an investigation had he conducted? Had he not read either Ellis's article in *Inside* magazine, or *The New Yorker* article about Ellis? In the *Inside* article, Ellis said that about 5:30 in the afternoon of Election Day, he took a smoke break and called "Governor Bush" (not specifying which governor), who asked Ellis, "Is it really this close?" Ellis responded, "Yeah, it's really close." (Ellis wrote that Bush had all of the VNS numbers already, though if that had been the case, one wonders why Bush would ask Ellis if it was "really" this close.) Later, after the networks called Florida for Gore, Ellis got a call from Jeb Bush. "Are you sure?" Bush asked about the Fox projection. "Jeb, I'm sorry, I'm looking at a screenful of Gore." Bush said, "But the polls haven't closed in the panhandle." Ellis replied, "It's not going to help."[18]

In an earlier interview with Jane Mayer of *The New Yorker*,[19] Ellis seemed even more candid, freely admitting that he had called his cousins and they had called him, so he could tell them what he was seeing on the VNS computer screens. Sometime after 6 P.M., according to Mayer, Ellis received a call from the Bush brothers. "They were, like, 'How we doin'?'" Ellis told Mayer. "I had to tell them it didn't look good." Later on it was Ellis who called his cousins, this time to give them good news. "Our projection shows that it is statistically impossible for Gore to win Florida," Ellis said. "Their mood was up big time." Then an hour later, Ellis again wanted to share VNS information with his cousins, this time to tell them he had just got a message on the computer screens that said the VNS numbers were wrong. "You gotta be kidding me," George W. Bush said.

One might assume that Ellis's several admissions that he related VNS data to his cousins would constitute at least one "shred" of evidence that Ailes says he was seeking—but maybe Ailes wasn't accepting un-coerced confessions as evidence.

IF THE HEARING accomplished nothing else, it solidified the perception that the whole problem for the Election Night 2000 fiasco could be attributed solely to VNS and not to the networks' decision desks. This spin benefited almost everyone involved. It implicitly let the networks off the hook, because it meant they were simply the victims of bad data. It excused the Fox, NBC, and CNN/CBS decision desks for rushing to judgment, as well as the ABC executive for overriding the network's decision desk. And it took the heat off Ellis and Fox by making it appear that the Florida call for Bush was legitimate. But ultimately the spin was wrong. There were, of course, problems with the VNS system, and with the data that were provided to the VNS subscribers. And certainly the first Florida call that projected Gore the winner was the "fault" of VNS, though all of the VNS procedures that led to that miscall had long been approved of by the networks. But blame for the second Florida miscall, which announced Bush as the next president of the United States, falls squarely on the networks' decision desks.

One might have expected the VNS editorial director to defend his operation to the press, but immediately after the election, the VNS board of directors (controlled by the networks) clamped a gag order on all of the VNS employees. The networks treated their organization as though it were an independent entity that all by itself had destroyed their reputation for news accuracy. They barely acknowledged that in fact they had organized and staffed the organization, and had a board that oversaw its operation. If there were serious problems with VNS in its performance, the networks were clearly responsible to a very significant degree. But VNS was a useful scapegoat, a way for the networks to distance themselves from the problems they had created. The gag order was useful in preventing the people who knew best what had happened from explaining the events to the public and contradicting the networks' spin. (The irony of this suppression of news by the television news organizations seemed lost on the network executives.) As an AP report notes, "VNS has issued two public statements but would not make its executives available for comment." It quoted title VNS Editorial Director Murray Edelman explaining why he could not comment on what happened: "There's a congressional investigation, there's a lawsuit pending. . . . It's a pretty inflamed subject right now," and VNS doesn't want to "pour any more kerosene on it."[20]

While VNS executives had to restrain themselves, that did not prevent the network executives from pouring kerosene. Dan Rather perhaps did it most dramatically, "As far as I'm concerned," he told radio commentator Don Imus, "we have to knock it [VNS] down to absolute ground zero, plow it under with salt, put a barbed-wire fence around it, quarantine it for a few years and start off with something new."[21] All the network executives added their threats to the continued operation of VNS, promising to review the organization's performance on election night and implying that it alone had caused the fiasco.

So effective was this effort in projecting an image of VNS incompetence that in his opening comments at the congressional hearings on February 14, 2001, U.S. Representative Edward J. Markey (D-Massachusetts) echoed the conventional wisdom: "The problem, in my view, is not with the network news divisions or their anchors . . . but rather with VNS. It is clear this flawed methodology and resulting shoddy VNS data misled the network news divisions and caused many of the problems for the networks and their election night coverage."[22]

Had Edelman been allowed to speak, he might have suggested that there had been data errors in all previous years, predictable in magnitude, and that he had explicitly warned the network decision teams about the size of such potential errors. He might also have reminded everyone that VNS did not make the disastrous Florida call for Bush, that the networks had made it on their own despite his advice to the contrary. But that is exactly what the networks did not want Edelman to say. And so they shut him up until the following May, by which time the story was old and VNS permanently tarred with the blame.

ONE REASON THE spin about VNS culpability was so successful is that there were in fact serious problems with the VNS system that needed to be addressed. In December 2000, the VNS board of directors contracted with Research Triangle Institute (RTI), a non-profit research organization in North Carolina, to undertake a thorough review of the VNS procedures. At the congressional hearing, Paul Biemer, the team leader of six senior statisticians and survey methodologists assembled by RTI, presented the major findings of the research.[23] None of the six individuals had any connection with VNS or any experience with the Election Day voting process. "This apparently was a key requirement of the VNS board for selecting RTI for the review," Biemer said, "and ensured an objective and impartial assessment of VNS operations."[24]

The RTI research team found four types of "system errors" that contributed to the erroneous calls in Florida, and several other areas where the VNS system could be improved.

One of the most serious errors was the incorrect estimate of the number of people who had voted early or by absentee ballot. This was not an issue when the system was first developed for CBS by Warren Mitofsky in the 1960s and 1970s, but over the years more states were allowing early and absentee votes, making it difficult for the election night projection system to make projections.

Another was the election model that compared vote patterns in the 2000 race with the patters in the 1998 gubernatorial race. It would have been better if the model had compared the 2000 presidential race with the 1996 presidential race. At the very least, the system needed to show comparisons between 2000 and both the 1996 and 1998 statewide races, but the software programs were not capable of doing that.

A third area was the estimate of the number of votes yet to be counted. The system was too simplistic and significantly underestimated the size of the outstanding vote. More use needed to be made of the vote histories, to ensure a more accurate projection of how many votes were likely to be cast.

The fourth area was the accuracy of vote tabulations from the county reports. That night there were several errors in the report of vote counts that could have been avoided, or at least detected, with better quality-control procedures. In the future it would be helpful if each data entry were displayed in the computer, so the analyst could review the record to see if there were any unusual entries that might signify an error.

Apart from these system errors, there was also an error in the calculation of the statistic that was used to measure how accurate an estimate was. This statistic, essentially a "margin of error" calculation, tells the analyst the probability that a projection will be wrong. The standard rule of thumb is that analysts will not call a race unless there is only one chance in two hundred that the call will be wrong. Some people want absolute certainty, such as one chance in a billion of being wrong, but the VNS system has always used the 1:200 ratio as the guideline. The RTI evaluation, however, showed that the formulas that were used to compute the ratio tended to underestimate the probability of being wrong when there was incomplete data. The error had been in the system since it was originally developed, but it had always been so small that it never had the impact that it did on Election Night 2000. The result was that early in the evening, "the risk that an election analyst will call an election erroneously could be substantially higher than indicated by the information on the decision screens."[25]

Representative Edward J. Markey glommed onto this quotation and other assessments of error in the VNS system to lay all the blame on VNS for the miscalls and to exonerate the networks.[26] He seemed particularly insistent that RTI's Paul Biemer agree with that view, though Biemer was reluctant to jump to that conclusion, not knowing what other information the decision teams had.

MARKEY: In other words, VNS is at fault here, not the network news divisions. They were sending up faulty information without giving the actual degree of true uncertainty as pointed out here that existed in the information as it was being presented. Isn't that accurate?

BIEMER: I don't know who's at fault, but I will say the statement we made there about the decision screens being misleading in terms of uncertainties, that is correct.

MARKEY: That is what I'm saying. So even if the information was accurately interpreted, it could have still led to erroneous conclusions; is that correct?

BIEMER: Yes.

MARKEY: Do you think the news directors would risk their careers based on something that could have led to erroneous conclusions, or do you think that VNS was the source of the problem and it wasn't properly communicated on the decision screens that there was in fact a much higher level of risk that was entailed in making projections based upon these numbers?

BIEMER: One of things we did not get into is what . . . their approach was for calling these elections. All we did was look into what procedures VNS used to produce these estimates, to collect the data, and put it on the decision screens. What happens after that we don't know.

MARKEY: Exactly. The point I am making here is the news anchors don't have Ph.D.s in statistics. VNS failed them—VNS did not give them the information in a form that was usable that would protect the reputations of the news divisions. Don't you agree with that?

BIEMER: I don't know if I agree or not because I don't know what information they got other than what's on the decision screens.

MARKEY: You say right here in your report—you say in your report, sir, you say "measures of uncertainty presented on the decision screens sent to the networks eliminates some potentially important sources of error in the VNS system and thus the true uncertainty." So you're saying that they sent erroneous information.

BIEMER: If they're only using the information on the decision screens, they are being misled.

· · ·

MARKEY: Do you understand what we are trying to do here, sir?

BIEMER: Yes.

MARKEY: We are trying to put the queen of spades in front of someone. I believe the queen of spades should sit right in front of VNS. I think there was obviously a terrible set of mistakes that were made at VNS that were then sent on to all of these other people who depended upon them. . . . So once VNS makes the mistake, everyone who's dependent upon it is going to be prone to looking pretty silly because they believe the numbers are accurate.

THE PROBLEMS IN the VNS system that Biemer outlined did in fact lead to the early projection of Gore as the winner in Florida, but that miscall had relatively little effect on news coverage and it was rescinded within two hours. In the interim, the networks continued to portray the national presidential contest as competitive, indicating that Bush could still win the presidency even if he lost Florida. It was the second miscall in Florida that created the political havoc, and that error cannot be blamed on VNS, despite Markey's and the networks' considerable efforts to make it appear that way. Even Biemer admitted later during the hearings that the VNS data at 2:15 in the morning, as erroneous as the data might have been, did not justify the Bush projection. Biemer's comments came in response to questions by Representative Sherrod Brown (D-Ohio) about the proprietary of Fox's employing Ellis to call the elections, given Ellis's family ties to the Bush brothers, and whether that family relationship might have affected the Fox call.

BROWN: Mr. Biemer, do you have an opinion?

BIEMER: Well, all I want to really point out is that . . . when the Bush call was made there was only like a .6 percentage point difference between the candidates. And *VNS did not make the Bush call, the networks did*. But looking at the data on the screen, I would not have made that call. So I don't know what happened in terms of calling it for Bush. *The data didn't support the call* as far as I'm concerned.

BROWN: So it may not be out of the question that the calls to Austin . . . could have possibly had an impact, or the American public could think they had an impact, on Fox making a decision that VNS really didn't suggest that they make?

BIEMER: I guess anything is possible. I don't understand why the call was made is all I would say.

Brown had come closer to the truth than anyone at the hearing could have known. The calls to Austin did have an impact on the Fox projection. Fox made the call, because Jeb Bush persuaded his cousin, John Ellis, to do so. NBC made the call because Sheldon Gawiser and his decision team saw Fox make it. CNN and CBS made the call because Warren Mitofsky said, "We'll do it, too!" when he heard the NBC projection. And ABC made the call because a network executive didn't trust his own decision team's conclusion—the same conclusion made by the independent RTI research team, and by the VNS editorial director, and by the Associated Press: *the data didn't support the call.*

On November 7, 2000, tens of thousands of eligible Florida voters were wrongly prevented from casting their ballots . . . Nearly all were Democrats, nearly half of them African-American. The systematic program that disfranchised these legal voters [was] directed by the offices of Florida's Governor Jeb Bush and Secretary of State Katherine Harris. . . . This little twist in the voter purge cost Al Gore a good 30,000 votes.

—*Greg Palast*, The Best Democracy Money Can Buy
February 5, 2001

■

Greg Palast distorts and misrepresents the events surrounding the 2000 presidential election in Florida in order to support his twisted and maniacally partisan conclusions.

—*Katherine Harris, Florida secretary of state, April 2002*

■

In a world where all perspectives are treated as equals, the truth becomes merely one more conjecture.

—*Lance deHaven-Smith,*The Battle for Florida

■

7

Theft of the Election

Jeb Bush's success in persuading his cousin to project George W. Bush the winner in Florida, though the data did not support the call, must have stunned the Florida governor. He could not possibly have known that Fox's call would trigger the other networks to make the same mistake, nor that the resulting political environment would be so instrumental in George Bush's eventual victory. No doubt Jeb Bush expected the call to be helpful, but that it turned out so much better than he could possibly have imagined was simple serendipity. And unlike many of his other successful actions to deprive selected blacks and poor people of the right to vote, Jeb Bush's sweet-talking his cousin John Ellis into making the miscall was not illegal or even in the realm of "dirty tricks." It was mere political opportunism that almost no politician would have turned down.

It remains unclear what Jeb Bush knew about the actual vote count in Florida and when he knew it. Shortly before the Fox call, the AP vote count showed George Bush's lead actually declining, with mostly Democratic counties yet to report their results. At 1:02 A.M. ET, Bush led by over 112,000 votes; at 1:31 A.M. ET, his lead was down to less than 60,000 votes. At 2:12, four minutes before Ellis made the call, the AP count showed Bush down to a 48,000-vote lead, and four minutes later it dropped just over 30,000 votes.[1] The notion that Jeb Bush might be aware of these declining counts comes from Ellis himself. "Jeb was wired into Florida," he wrote, and provided "very useful information" about "which precincts [in Florida] had yet to report and how those precincts had voted in Jeb's prior gubernatorial races."[2] Indeed, it was Jeb Bush's connection to Florida that gave Ellis such confidence that when Jebbie said "We got it," Jebbie knew what he was talking about. If Ellis is right, and Bush was in fact wired into the actual vote count in Florida, the Florida governor might well have known about the diminishing lead for George Bush and urged his cousin to make the call precisely because of the decline.

Still, whether Jeb Bush actually believed his brother would win, or was manipulating his cousin to believe it in the hopes of obtaining some small media advantage, is a relatively trivial distinction. Jeb Bush's actions that night were part of a much broader and sustained effort to help his brother become president of the United States, including some actions that were legal and others that were not. After six years and many unofficial investigations and reports into what happened in Florida both before and after election 2000, the evidence seems overwhelming that the presidential election of 2000 was stolen—with participation by, at the very least, Jeb Bush's office, Florida Secretary of State Katherine Harris's office, some Florida Republicans and other supporters, and ultimately by a majority of the Supreme Court. This theft of the election does not have to be seen as a grand conspiracy among the various actors. Many of the actions were uncoordinated, many accidental, though clearly some actions were part and parcel of a larger general effort to deprive blacks and poor people, mostly Democrats, of their right to vote.

Some of the most damning evidence was initially revealed by Greg Palast, an American reporter for two British newspapers, *The Guardian* of London and its Sunday sister paper, *The Observer*, and for BBC-TV's

Newsnight. A review of his findings is chronicled in the 2004 edition of *The Best Democracy Money Can Buy.*[3] His investigations reached some stunning conclusions.

Several months before the 2000 election, Florida's secretary of state, Katherine Harris, ordered 57,700 voters to be purged from the voter rolls on the grounds that they were felons (had been convicted of a felony at some point in their lives) and were not entitled to vote. The company hired by Florida to generate this purge list, Data Base Technologies (DBT), which has since merged into ChoicePoint, first reviewed selected databases that included felons from Florida and other states, and then matched those names against people on the Florida voter rolls. The matching criteria included names, date of birth, and gender, with the race data provided for final comparison by the county election officials.

As it turns out, Palast notes, more than 90 percent of Florida voters on that purge list should not have been there. Either they had committed only a misdemeanor and not a felony, had committed a felony but their voting rights had been restored by the state where they were convicted (and thus Florida could not bar them from voting), or had committed no crime but had just been wrongly matched.

The two major problems causing this humongous error rate were 1) the lack of verification, and 2) the deliberate effort of DBT to include "more names than were actually verified as being a convicted felon."[4] Both of those problems could be laid directly at the feet of the Florida secretary of state's office. The instructions from the state to DBT were to have an 80 percent match of the names, not a perfect match. In some cases, even the birth dates did not agree.

At a congressional hearing in early 2001, a vice president at Choice-Point, James Lee, admitted that DBT deliberately allowed the errors because state officials had told the firm to do so. "The list of voters DBT supplied to the state [to be used to delete felons] did include the names of people who were eligible to vote," Lee said. "The state officials knew this would be the result."[5] He went on to say that his firm proposed to the state that DBT use several additional databases—such as property tax lists, telephone number lists, and change of address lists—in order to "reduce the numbers of eligible voters included on the list."[6] But Florida officials did not want to do that.[7] Instead, this was a deliberate effort to get more people on the list than could be identified as felons. And those people were disproportionately black.

Lee's testimony was reinforced by the sworn testimony of George Bruder, a vice president of DBT, who appeared before the U.S. Civil Rights Commission during its hearings in Florida, in January and February 2001. Bruder also admitted that DBT knew there were many mismatches in the list, but that the Florida Division of Elections wanted the mismatches. In fact, the Division of Elections said that matches should be allowed even when the last names of the felons only approximated the last names of the Florida voters, and that the first and middle names did not have to be in the same order. Thus, a felon named John Andrew Smith would be considered a match with a voter named John Andrew Smythe, Andrew John Smith, Andrew John Smythe, John Adrew Smittt, Andrew John Smitt, Drew Smith, Jon Smith, and so on. As Bruder testified, "The state dictated to us that they wanted to go broader and we did it in the fashion they requested."[8]

THE CONTRACT BETWEEN Florida and DBT specified that the firm was required to verify all the matches between known felons and Florida voters. The method was "manual verification using telephone calls and statistical sampling."[9] But Palast discovered that "with the state's blessing, DBT did not call a single felon." Eventually even Harris admitted that Palast's charge was correct. "We provided this 'blessing,'" she wrote, "at the behest of Florida's county supervisors of elections who wished to contact the persons on the list themselves, pursuant to their statutory responsibility."[10] But, as Palast notes,

Harris never explained why DBT was paid $2.3 million to verify names, though it never did the verification. Also, "Harris's apocryphal claim that county officials asked to take over this expensive work," Palast writes, "counters both the correspondence in her files and my own conversations with the county election supervisors."[11]

Jeb Bush's office also took steps to illegally deprive tens of thousands of Florida citizens of their legal right to vote. On September 18, 2000, six weeks before the election, the governor's Office of Executive Clemency sent a letter to the Division of Elections, notifying it that felons "whose civil rights were restored automatically by statute in the state of conviction" would still have to apply for the "restoration of civil rights in Florida."[12] That order was in direct violation of two Florida Supreme Court rulings, which declared that according to state law and the U.S. Constitution, a felon whose voting rights had been restored in the state where he was convicted could not be deprived of his voting rights in Florida. Nor could the state require the felon to apply for clemency in Florida, the purpose of which was to restore rights the felon already had. Despite the clear rulings by the court, Jeb Bush's office simply ignored the ruling and ordered the Division of Elections to bar such felons from voting. The estimated number of felons who would otherwise have been entitled to vote was between 40,000 and 80,000.[13]

Did Jeb Bush personally know about the illegal letter and efforts to prevent out-of-state felons from exercising their right to vote? According to Palast, a clerk in Bush's office suggested that the Florida governor did know, that while the court told Bush not to interfere with ex-cons who had voting rights, he deliberately did it anyway.[14]

Shortly after the election, and just a week after the U.S. Civil Rights Commission began investigating the matter, the governor's Office of Executive Clemency wrote another letter—this one rescinding the instructions sent out before the election. Giving the impression that there was no change, the letter began by saying, "Some confusion has recently arisen regarding the effect of out-of-state restoration of civil rights on former felons' civil rights in Florida. To correct any misunderstanding, this letter reiterates our current policy." The letter then directly contradicts its September orders by saying that felons whose voting rights have been restored in another state "need not apply for restoration of civil rights in Florida."[15] In the meantime, thousands of voters had been denied the opportunity to vote in the 2000 presidential election.

Who were the voters who were denied their lawful voting rights by Jeb Bush's letter and by Katherine Harris's purge lists? Overwhelmingly, they were blacks and poorer whites. Assuming that voting turnout among the barred voters would have been about the same as the rest of the Florida voters, and that the barred voters would have cast their ballots in roughly the same pattern as other voters of the same race and socioeconomic status, Palast estimates that Gore would have picked up a net 30,000 votes more than George W. Bush. Given that Gore lost Florida by just 537 votes, Gore's winning margin would have been more than 29,000 votes. Even if one made much more conservative estimates about the turnout or voting patterns of the barred voters, there is almost no way Bush could have won the election if those tens of thousands of voters had not been illegally barred from casting a ballot.

Perhaps one reason why the theft of election 2000 is not more dramatically clear is that there are some probabilities tied to all of the estimates. How many of the incorrectly purged voters would actually have turned out to vote had they been able to? How many of the felons who had been illegally barred from voting would have turned out to vote if they had not been barred from registering in the first place? And for both groups, how would they have voted? The answers to those questions involve some degree of guesswork, and that's why despite the large numbers, observers tend to be cautious in interpreting the results. But Gore needed to overcome only 537 votes, and any reasonable projection of turnout and voting preferences would show Gore winning Florida by thousands of votes. In legal terms, we can be sure that Gore would have won the election *beyond a reasonable doubt*.

IN 2005, A LONG-TIME student of Florida politics and a highly respected analyst of Florida politics, Professor Lance deHaven Smith of Florida State University, published a book with his own examination of the 2000 election in Florida. He, too, discovered much that was rotten in the state of Florida. He notes that "the acts of subterfuge and sabotage committed by Katherine Harris, Jeb Bush, Tom Feeney, and other Republicans" were not aberrations, but "business as usual."[16] While the felon disenfranchisement program was mandated by state law, he writes, it was "corrupted" by Harris when she implemented it, including her insistence that DBT "use loose criteria that would cause many eligible voters to be improperly identified as ex-felons."[17] Like Palast, he concluded that "by itself, the felon disenfranchisement program probably cost Gore the election. Not only did it cut into Democratic voting strength, it also resulted in massive confusion on Election Day when poll workers told many voters that they were no longer eligible to cast a ballot. Confusion and disorder was rampant at polling places serving black and low-income neighborhoods."[18]

DeHaven-Smith also refers to an illegal letter sent by Jeb Bush to Republicans urging them to vote absentee, which was apparently designed to increase turnout among members of his party. But the letter was illegal on two counts. First, it used official stationery bearing the state seal, as though this were an official communication from the governor's office instead of a campaign flyer. Second, it urged Republican voters to do what was contrary to the law at the time—vote absentee simply because it was more convenient than voting on Election Day. The law at the time required that specific circumstances be met for absentee voting, not just that it was more convenient. The Florida Democratic Party obtained a court injunction to stop the letters' use.[19]

This action is a relatively minor abuse of office, compared with the denial of felons' right to vote, but it reinforces the perception that the governor and his top aides appeared willing to violate the law if they could get away with it. DeHaven-Smith also cites other actions by Jeb Bush in the post-election period that "appear to have been violations of Florida law." Among other things, Bush "instructed or, at the very least, allowed his legal staff, while they too were working on state time, to contact the state's biggest law firms and discourage them from working for Gore." The problem here is not only was this a misappropriation of state resources for partisan purposes, the law firms that were contacted had state contracts and lobbying contracts that required access to the governor. Thus, the calls from Bush's office could very easily have been, or certainly could have been perceived as being, veiled threats.[20]

DeHaven-Smith cites numerous other potentially illegal actions by Bush and Harris, whose official responsibilities were "to administer the election process to assure fairness," but who were instead "seeking to prevent the votes cast on Election Day from being fully and fairly counted, even though, or precisely because, they realized that careful review might show that Gore had won."[21] The summer after the election, *The New York Times* reported what appeared to be a conspiracy among Florida officials, the military, and some congressional Republicans, which encouraged military personnel to vote after Election Day and ensured their votes would be counted, in violation of state law.[22]

Still, the Florida scholar recognized that corrupt politics is an integral part of American history. And when corruption is widespread, it usually triggers some serious reform. But that did not happened after election 2000. "What alarmed me was not the malfeasance and misfeasance of high officials," he wrote, "but rather the inability of both the public and the media to see what was happening and, worse, their widespread reluctance, later, to conduct a postmortem of the election fiasco."[23]

He could understand why Republicans would not want to pursue the subject, but he could not understand the silence of Democrats or the news media. To some extent the sudden drop in attention could be attributed to what Greg Palast called "Al Gore's despicably gracious concession speech."[24] After all, if the Democratic candidate had accepted the result, why shouldn't the media? Whatever the reason, "Immediately after the inauguration, the media dropped the issue like a stinky diaper."[25] There were a few stories in the spring and summer of the following year, but as is the media's wont, the findings were treated as partisan disputes, with little effort to pinpoint the truth. "Consequently," deHaven-Smith writes, "even though the articles contained circumstantial evidence of malfeasance and felonious crimes by Florida officials at the highest levels, and of election fraud involving the military and perhaps members of Congress, they never generated much attention."[26]

Neither did the Democrats do anything to investigate the election problems, even after May 24, 2001, when Vermont's Republican Senator James Jeffords left the GOP to give Democrats majority control of the U.S. Senate, and thus the power to initiate congressional investigations. The only significant effort to investigate alleged crimes was made by the U.S. Civil Rights Commission. In January and February 2001, deHaven-Smith writes, it found evidence of "a possible conspiracy by Florida's Republican Secretary of State and other high-ranking Republican officials, perhaps including Florida Governor Jeb Bush" to illegally purge Democratic voters from the Florida rolls,[27] the crime that Greg Palast has documented in great detail. But like other reports and news articles, the commission findings were tarred with charges of partisanship, and no effort was made by any governmental or news media organization to verify the truth. "In a world where all perspectives are treated as equals," writes the Florida scholar, "the truth becomes merely one more conjecture."[28]

THE THEFT OF tens of thousands of votes by Jeb Bush, Katherine Harris, and other Republicans was not sufficient to give George Bush a victory in Florida. It merely made Gore's margin very small, as we know now from the news media consortium's count of the vote—Gore winning by anywhere from 42 to 171 votes. Bush also needed a deus ex machina to complete the theft, which took the form of an intervention by the United States Supreme Court. Not all constitutional scholars or law professors agree that the Court "hijacked" the election, as Harvard Professor Alan Dershowitz argues,[29] or that the Supreme Court "betrayed America," as charged by former Los Angeles Prosecutor Vincent Bugliosi.[30] Still, an inordinate number reacted with shock at the Court's decision. "Never before in American history," Dershowitz writes, "have so many law professors, historians, political scientists, Supreme Court litigators, journalists who cover the high court, and other experts—at all points along the political spectrum—been in agreement that the majority decision of the Court was not only 'bad constitutional law' but 'lawless,' 'illegitimate,' 'unprincipled,' 'partisan,' 'fraudulent,' 'disingenuous,' and motivated by improper considerations."[31]

On January 13, 2001, 554 law professors signed a protest that was published in a *New York Times* advertisement, and then later posted on a Web site. Eventually the list of signers included what Bugliosi called "an astonishing" 673 law professors from around the country. The ad read: "We are professors of law at 137 American law schools, from every part of our country, of different political beliefs. But we all agree that when a bare majority of the U.S. Supreme Court halted the recount of ballots under Florida law, the five justices were acting as political proponents for candidate Bush, not as judges." Perhaps the most relevant charge they leveled at the Court was that "the conservative justices moved to avoid the 'threat' that Americans might learn that in the recount, Gore got more votes than Bush."[32]

While various scholars have made numerous arguments against the Court's decision, perhaps the four most compelling points are the following:

1. Bogus Deadline

The contest for the presidency ended on December 12, 2000, not because the Supreme Court found fault with Gore's request of a hand recount, but because the Court said there was not enough time to establish satisfactory recount rules and still conduct the recount. The Court determined that the deadline for any such recount was December 12; the Court issued its opinion at 10:00 P.M. that same day, leaving less than two hours, which the Court felt was not enough time to conduct a full statewide recount.

But the deadline was bogus. Federal law does not require the electoral process to be completed by December 12. In fact, as noted by Jed Rubenfeld, a Yale University law professor, "Most of the states in this election [election 2000] submitted their electoral votes *after* December 12."[33] That date is a "safe harbor" date, which as Temple University law professor David Kairys notes "is not a deadline for determining a state's electors, as the Bush campaign and most of the media viewed it, but the date after which a state's electors could be potentially subject to challenge in Congress. A state's electors can be designated, in theory, at any time prior to the Electoral College vote."[34] In fact, Rubenfeld writes, in a similarly tight contest in Hawaii in 1960, a state court ordered a recount of the presidential vote after the state initially certified Richard Nixon the winner by ninety-eight votes. Nixon supporters protested that the recount could not be completed by the safe harbor date, but the court disregarded the protests. Though John Kennedy was certified the winner by 115 votes on December 28, well after the safe harbor date, that did not prevent Hawaii's electoral votes from being counted in favor of Kennedy.[35]

Because *federal* law does not set a deadline of December 12, the five majority justices in *Bush v. Gore* tried to make it appear that Florida *state* law mandated such a deadline. But it did not. And the five justices knew it. "How then did the majority come up with a December 12 deadline?" asks Professor Rubenfeld. "The opinion says only one thing on this crucial point, and what it says defies the credibility of a child . . . The majority said that they had to honor the December 12 deadline out of deference to . . . the Florida Supreme Court." That was an astounding ruling for these justices, who had found fault with almost everything else the Florida Supreme Court had done. But even in this reference, the Supreme Court justices were playing fast and loose with language. The Florida Supreme Court had not set a deadline, but ordered the recount to proceed "forthwith." The Florida court did say that Florida law was designed to allow Florida to "participate fully in the federal electoral process," which the Supreme Court then, by a major leap in logic, decided meant December 12, the safe harbor deadline. "This passage—on which the entire decision turns—is not merely unpersuasive," Professor Rubenfeld writes. "It is deceptive and indefensible."[36] He concludes: "There was no December 12 deadline. The majority made it up. On this pretense, the presidential election was determined."[37] A *New York Times* columnist, Thomas Friedman, perhaps best characterized the significance of the Court's ruling: "The five conservative Justices essentially ruled that the sanctity of dates, even meaningless ones, mattered more than the sanctity of votes, even meaningful ones."[38]

2. Selective Application of "Equal Protection of the Law"

On December 12, the Supreme Court ruled that the hand recount ordered by the Florida Supreme Court violated the equal protection clause of the Fourteenth Amendment to the U.S. Constitution. The only standard for counting the votes provided by state law was "the clear intent of the voter." The Bush brief argued that this was insufficient, because of the variation in county standards as to what constituted voter intent: "A partially punched ballot, for example, may not be counted at all in most counties, might be counted as a vote in other counties, and in some counties it might be counted as a vote or not."[39]

Even some critics of the Court's final decision in *Bush v. Gore* admitted that this argument had some theoretical legal merit, but if so, then it should also have applied to the original vote count. If the Supreme Court felt the recount was flawed because of the various standards used by county officials, writes Bugliosi, "then to be completely consistent the Court would have had no choice but to invalidate the entire Florida election, since there is no question that votes lost in some counties because of the method of voting would have been recorded in others utilizing a different method."[40]

Indeed the method of voting differed substantially from county to county. Some counties used the Votomatic punch-card system, while others used an optical-scan system. These clearly did not provide "equal" systems: the Votomatic system produced more than twice as many no-vote errors as did the optical-scan system.[41]

In Palm Beach was another and infamous inequality. There, the so-called "butterfly" ballot alone cost Gore the election. It was a special design, different from the rest of the ballots in the state, with the candidates on the two open pages facing the voter. On the left side of the page, the top two listed candidates were Bush and Gore, but the hole that had to be punched for Gore was the *third* hole from the top, not the second one. The second hole from the top, located in the middle of the two-page ballot, was for Buchanan—the top-listed candidate on the second page. Many voters were confused by this design, thinking they were voting for Gore but actually voting for Buchanan. Thousands of them punched the second hole—which was for Buchanan—but then wrote in Gore's name. All those votes were invalidated as "overvotes"—because more than one candidate was selected. According to the *Palm Beach Post*, which conducted a post-election review of all of the votes actually cast, Gore lost a net 6,607 votes because of that faulty design.[42] A statistical study conducted by university scholars who focused just on the number of ballots that were actually recorded concluded that the butterfly ballot "caused more than 2,000 Democratic voters to vote by mistake for Reform candidate Pat Buchanan."[43] Add to that the net loss of votes *not* counted, and Gore would have won in Florida by more than 8,000 votes had the ballot design in Palm Beach been the same as in most other counties. Clearly, allowing one county to have this different kind of design violated the "equal protection" clause.

Overvotes were also a major problem in Duval County, where the unique ballot design was as much of a problem as the butterfly ballot in Palm Beach. The Duval ballot required voters to turn to the second page to see all presidential candidates. In a sample ballot widely circulated and published in the newspapers just before the election, the instructions emphasized that the voters should vote on "every page" of the ballot. But in voting on every page, voters would be voting for more than one candidate and thus invalidating their ballot—another example of "overvoting." This design alone, according to a post-election analysis by *USA Today* and Knight-Ridder, probably cost Gore some 2,600 votes.[44]

Also in Florida, different counties used different criteria for deciding which voters were legal voters, and they also used different standards for accepting absentee ballots—with some counties accepting absentee votes after the official Florida deadline for such ballots, and other counties rejecting such absentee votes.[45]

All of these discrepancies had come to the attention of the Supreme Court, noted Professor Rubenfeld, "but no one of these other disparities and inequalities—all of which favored Bush, and every one of which involved a disputed number of votes potentially large enough to alter the election—was dealt with by the Supreme Court or any other court in terms of the equal protection reasoning announced in *Bush v. Gore*."[46]

And there was another crucial problem in the equal protection ruling—the lack of a victim. Unlike the inequalities just described, which all caused Gore's support to be undercounted, if there were different standards applied in hand counting the ballots, there was no evidence that either Bush or Gore would be the more disadvantaged. "In other cases," Harvard's Alan Dershowitz writes, "Justice Scalia would be all over the lawyers, demanding to know who it was that was being denied equal protection of the law. But in this case, neither Scalia nor his colleagues appeared to be troubled by the absence of a victim." Dershowitz concludes that the real victim in this case "were the voters whose ballots were valid under Florida law, but whose votes were never counted because of the Supreme Court's decision."[47]

3. "Limited to the Present Circumstances"

After announcing their decision in *Bush v. Gore,* the five conservative justices added that their rationale for the decision "is limited to the present circumstances." This meant that while the "kooky" reasoning of the Court about the equal protection law could be applied to the Florida recount, such reasoning would not be applied to other elections.[48] And for good reason. Professor Kairys notes that if the principles stated by the Court were applied consistently, not only would they "invalidate the entire Florida electoral system," they would also invalidate the electoral systems in many states and much of the federal system."[49]

One might have predicted that the justice most opposed to this type of unique ruling would have been Justice Antonin Scalia, whose repeated writings and judgments argued against deciding cases without establishing precedents for future courts to follow. In a 1996 case, Scalia wrote:

> The Supreme Court of the United States does not sit to announce "unique" dispositions. Its principal function is to establish precedent—that is to set forth principles of law that every court in America must follow. . . . We expect both ourselves and lower courts to adhere to the "rationale upon which the Court based the results of its earlier decisions." . . . That is the principal reason we publish our opinions.[50]

But in this case, Scalia did not attempt to set forth principles of law that every court could follow. "What he did in this case cannot be justified by any acceptable standard of judicial behavior," writes Professor Dershowitz. "He . . . decided the case not on neutral principles or precedents designed to govern future cases, but rather on the basis of whom sic he wanted to see win this election."[51] That judgment applies to all of the five justices voting in the majority: "Their votes reflected not any enduring constitutional values rooted in the precedents of the ages, but rather the partisan quest for immediate political victory. In so voting, they shamed themselves and the Court on which they serve, and they defiled their places in history."[52]

4. Continued Vote Recount Would Cause "Irreparable Harm" to Bush

On Friday, December 8, 2001, in response to an appeal by Gore, the Florida Supreme Court adjusted the total vote count by allowing some votes for Gore that had been denied by the secretary of state's office. As reported by Jeffrey Toobin in *Too Close to Call*,[53] that left Bush with a lead of just 154 votes. More important, a majority of the Florida Supreme Court, by a 4-to-3 decision, ordered a statewide recount of all undervotes. For weeks, the Republicans had been criticizing Gore for demanding hand recounts in just a few highly Democratic counties, a "selective" approach that, they argued, undermined his call for letting all votes count. The Republicans were not about to retaliate by asking for recounts in highly Republican counties, however, because that would legitimize Gore's request for a hand recount. The criticism was intended to show the hypocrisy of the Gore strategy, without having to accept the principle of recount. But the Florida Supreme Court took note of the Republican criticisms and wrote, "We agree with the [Republicans] that the ultimate relief would require a counting of the legal votes contained within the undervotes in all counties where the undervote has not been subjected to a manual retabulation."[54] With the undervotes already hand tabulated in three counties, the court's majority ordered recounts in the remaining sixty-four counties.

Judge Terry Lewis was given the task of supervising the recount of 60,000 or so undervotes from across the state. Late Friday night, he ordered the process to begin on Saturday morning, December 9, and to be completed by Sunday afternoon at 2:00 P.M. Judges from across the political spectrum volunteered to oversee the vote counts in each of the counties. Each pair of judges was observed by county workers and by one observer from each party. The Bush team had objected to the recount on the grounds that there were no statewide standards for determining whether a ballot should be counted, but Judge Lewis instructed the judges to make the determination by the only criterion already in the statutes: "the clear intent of the voter." He wanted that standard applied strictly. "If in doubt, throw it out," he told them. In each county, a pair of judges would examine every ballot. If the two judges agreed on voter intent, they would count the vote. Otherwise they would put the card in a disputed pile, to be examined later by Judge Lewis. "In his decent and careful way, Terry Lewis had created a structure that could work—and was working," writes Toobin. "Quietly, efficiently, to be sure imperfectly, hundreds of people were making a better presidential election across the state of Florida on the morning of Saturday, December 9."[55]

In the meantime, the Bush lawyers had already appealed the decision to the U.S. Supreme Court, asking for a stay of the recount process and a reversal of the Florida court's decision. Justices Rehnquist, Scalia, Thomas, O'Connor ,and Kennedy agreed to the stay, with no justification offered. Still, any stay granted by the Court required the plaintiff to show that he would suffer "irreparable harm" if the stay were not granted. As Toobin notes, "The events of Saturday morning, December 9, made clear that the Bush campaign had no basis to show any irreparable harm. . . . The only possible 'harm' to Bush was the counting of Florida's votes."[56] Justice Stevens wrote a brief dissenting opinion on behalf of the four justices who were opposed to the stay. "Counting every legally cast vote cannot constitute irreparable harm [to Bush]. On the other hand, there is a danger that a stay may cause irreparable harm to [Gore] and, more importantly, the public at large. . . . Preventing the recount from being completed will inevitably cast a cloud on the legitimacy of the election."[57]

Shortly before the stay was issued, Justice Scalia wrote a three-paragraph opinion of his own, reflecting the majority vote. "The issuance of the stay suggests that a majority of the Court . . . believe that [George W. Bush] *has a substantial probability of success.*" He went on to say "the counting of votes that are of questionable legality does in my view threaten irreparable harm to [Bush], and to the country, by casting a cloud upon what *he claims to be the legitimacy of his election.*"[58] Only if the justices already perceived Bush to be the actual winner could they make the argument that irreparable harm would come to Bush by counting the votes. But that, according to Scalia, was precisely what the justices did think—despite the fact that all legally cast ballots had not been counted. Or, maybe the justices did not think that Bush had necessarily won; instead, as Dershowitz and others argue, perhaps the five justices didn't care (or want to know) who the real winner was and thus decided the case based not on principles but "on their political preferences."[59]

Whatever the motivation of the five justices, "The stark reality," writes Bugliosi, "is that the institution Americans trust the most to protect its freedoms and principles committed one of the biggest and most serious crimes the nation has ever seen—pure and simple, the theft of the presidency."[60]

SANDWICHED BETWEEN THE pre-election machinations that denied thousands of Democratic Floridians their right to vote and the post-election maneuvers that led to the Supreme Court's coup de grace are the events on Election Night 2000 reported in the first six chapters of this book. Viewed within this context, Jeb Bush's actions to persuade his cousin to call Florida for George Bush, though the data did not justify the call, are rather tame, a minor and unplanned part of a much broader effort by the Florida governor and many other Republicans to do whatever they could, with ethics and the law treated as mere inconveniences, to allow George W. Bush to win the presidency. Yet, oddly enough, without the networks' collective miscall, and the subsequent concession by Al Gore to George Bush, it's quite possible that the whole Bush/Harris/Republican effort to take the presidency would have failed.

After the automatic machine recount mandated by state law was completed (except for eighteen counties that did not do any machine recount), Gore trailed Bush by just 327 votes. The Democrat had just won a plurality of the national vote, and in any other modern democratic state would have won the election. The vote in Florida was so close, and reports of voting irregularities so widespread, that a hand recount—as is typically done in most states when the vote is so close— was a logical next step to ensure an accurate result. Thus, had Gore not already conceded the election (after the networks' miscall) and then subsequently un-conceded, the rallying cry of Republicans that Gore was a sore loser would not have been compelling, and certainly would have been far less likely to lead to the kind of negative media coverage for Gore that gripped the state. It's also possible that Gore and his staff would have adopted a different post-election strategy, pushing more aggressively for a full statewide recount of all the votes, as Gore personally favored, rather than trying to quickly gather enough votes in selected Democratic counties to counter his image as a sore loser trying to overturn the election. Had such an effort been made, it's quite possible that the Florida Supreme Court would have ruled earlier for such a recount, avoiding a premature ending of the recount by the U.S. Supreme Court.

It is also possible that at least one of the Supreme Court justices would not have become convinced that Bush was the real winner and that Gore was trying to steal the election, and thus may not have agreed to halting the vote count on the grounds of "irreparable harm" to Bush. The perception that Bush was the real winner, if indeed it influenced any judge, had to be the consequence of watching the news. In their post-election analyses of how the five U.S. Supreme Court justices came to their conclusions, Harvard Professors Alan Dershowitz and Lawrence Tribe suggest that the justices were in fact unduly influenced by television news. Tribe is widely regarded as the leading constitutional law professor in the country, and writes that "this succession of television images [media coverage of the post-election events in Florida] does more than represent the case of *Bush v. Gore*; it profoundly shaped the Supreme Court's understanding of the stakes involved and its ultimate holding that the Florida Supreme Court's December 8 order . . . violated the Fourteenth Amendment's equal protection clause."[61] Dershowitz also notes that during the post-election skirmishing for votes, "The Republicans scored a public-relations coup and even seemed to influence some of the justices, who apparently got their facts more from CNN than from the evidentiary record in the case."[62]

If television news could influence the justices on such technical matters as the application of the equal protection clause, the news would be even more likely to affect some of the justices' perceptions about the political situation—which in turn was profoundly shaped by the networks' miscall on election night. It's quite possible no amount of argument or news could have persuaded Justices Rehnquist, Scalia and Thomas to change their minds, all of whom by previous behavior had indicated their willingness to subordinate principle to outcome.[63] Still, it's not beyond the realm of imagination that either Justice O'Connor or Justice Kennedy may have been amenable to considering factors other than their own personal political preferences. Dershowitz is not sanguine that O'Connor was open to persuasion, but as noted earlier in this book, Justice Souter felt he might well have persuaded Kennedy if he'd had "just one more day" to discuss the issue.[64]

Still, whatever the ultimate impact of the networks' miscall on the Supreme Court decision, the projection of Bush as the next president of the United States, followed by Gore's concession and then his concession withdrawal, undoubtedly created an environment that was hostile to Gore's efforts to get what in almost any other election would have been considered a routine hand recount. That hostile environment no doubt also contributed to the public relief once the election had finally been decided, which was followed—as described by Lance deHaven-Smith—by a sudden silence following the inauguration. It was as though there had been no corruption of the election process itself, and the only changes needed were technical in nature—new and better voting machines, rather than a new and objective nonpartisan process for conducting fair elections.

In the end, George Bush's ascension to the presidency was highly improbable. It depended on Florida's wildly successful felon disenfranchisement program, which illegally deprived Gore of a net 20,000 to 30,000 votes on election night. It was aided by the serendipitous but stunning capitulation of the networks to the miscall by Fox and Jeb Bush, which created a hostile post-election political environment for Gore's efforts to obtain an accurate vote count in Florida. It was furthered by the partisan, unethical, and in many cases illegal efforts of top Florida officials to ensure a Bush victory, though they were sworn to serve all the people, not just voters of one party. And Bush's ascension to the presidency was finally assured by the unprecedented "corrupt"[65] and even "criminal"[66] intervention by the Supreme Court.

When most people talk about how the Republicans or the Supreme Court "stole" election 2000, they are looking at only one phase of the overall effort—the Supreme Court decision, or the political maneuvering in Florida after the election, or the pre-election felon disenfranchisement program prior to the election. Few if any focus on the overall picture, though to do so is to be convinced beyond a reasonable doubt that Election 2000 was indeed stolen.

A stock response to the new revelations in this book could be the one given by Ari Fleischer, George W. Bush's first White House press secretary, whenever reporters alluded to new evidence about the corruption of the Florida vote: "The nation, the president, and all but the most partisan Americans," he said, "have moved on."[67] Let's hope he is wrong. Living in ignorance, or in denial, about the past is the first step on the pathway to tyranny.

The exit polls were badly flawed. The exit poll numbers we have paid for and been provided simply do not add up.

—*Steve Coll, managing editor,* The Washington Post, *November 3, 2004*

We were ill-served.

—*Bill Keller, executive editor of* The New York Times, *demanding a partial refund of the fee paid to the exit poll operation conducted by Edison/Mitofsky, following Election 2004*

The exit polls got it flat wrong.

—*Charles Gibson, ABC's* Good Morning America, *November 3, 2004*

These were the same people who screwed up in 2000. Somewhere in the future this whole process must be completely changed, or even eliminated.

—National Review *Online, November 3, 2004*

The lesson here is put not your faith in exit polls.

—*Bill Schneider, CNN political commentator and former Harvard University political science professor, November 4, 2004*

8

Election 2004
Another Uproar

Election 2004 would be the first major test for the networks and their election night projection system since the disastrous miscalls of 2000. Once again, the election was expected to be close, some political observers even suggesting that this time it might be the Democratic candidate who would win the most electoral votes while losing the popular vote. After all the apologies and excuses the networks gave for their performance in 2000, they were determined not to commit the same errors this time. In 2000, being first won out at the expense of being right. This election, it would be different. This election, they would get it right.

At about three in the afternoon of Election Day 2004, Tuesday, November 2, I arrived at 34 W. Main Street, Somerville, New Jersey. Upstairs, in windowless offices, an array of computers on either side of two walls carried the results of thousands of polls across the country.[1] This was the headquarters of the new network consortium's exit poll operation, headed now by Warren Mitofsky and Joe Lenski, the CBS/CNN gurus I was with on Election Night 2000.

Mitofsky was sitting at one of the computers and turned around with a half grin on his face. "I can tell you right now what the headlines will be in the morning," he said without preamble or greeting. "Osama bin Laden Helps Kerry." It was the grin of someone who thinks he has a secret, a secret of great interest that few others know. And the secret he believed he had was that John Kerry would be the next president of the United States. As it turned out, that information wasn't a secret. Early results from the exit polls had metastasized on the Internet, so that anyone paying attention and surfing the Web already knew what Mitofsky thought he knew. But what everybody thought they knew was wrong.

DESPITE THE NETWORKS' blustering about VNS during the Congressional hearings in early 2001, the consortium members ultimately decided to keep with the operation they had founded. In doing so, however, they imposed stricter controls on the VNS staff and established oversight authority higher within the networks' hierarchies. Now a vice president in each network was officially in charge, although the steering committee remained the same—representatives from each news organization who were involved in their polling operations. The networks assigned a former CBS executive, Ted Savaglio, as the executive director in charge of the overall VNS operation. Murray Edelman, who had headed the election night projection system since 1994, kept that job, but with the title of editorial director.

To help upgrade the computer system for election night projections, the board hired the Battelle Memorial Institute in Columbus, Ohio. But it was a horrible choice. As Rich Morin of *The Washington Post* wrote, "VNS experienced serious problems with Battelle almost from the start of their relationship. . . . Consortium employees repeatedly warned the board that Battelle was failing to perform—warnings that the board did not take seriously, according to sources with direct knowledge of VNS operations."[2] Battelle didn't have the expertise to deal with the complexity of an operation that massive, and on election night the computer system failed completely. No exit poll data, and no actual vote counts from selected precincts, were available for network analysis.

Although it was clearly the fault of Battelle, a firm hired and directed by the board and not the VNS staff, it was the VNS staff who took the fall. On Tuesday, January 14, 2003, a Fox vice president, acting on behalf of the network consortium, had told the assembled VNS employees that the networks would close down VNS. "We had a really major embarrassment in 2000, and another in 2002," he told the employees. "We had to do something."[3]

Edelman was incensed. It was sheer "hypocrisy," he told me. "They [the networks] made us the scapegoat. We didn't make the miscall [projecting Bush the winner in Florida] in 2000, they did." And leading up to the 2002 election, he said, "We warned them about the problem . . . that Battelle was not getting it done, but they didn't listen. It was the networks who exercised control. When they fired VNS, they really fired themselves!"[4]

Edelman was only partially right about the warnings. The technical staff at VNS had indeed told the Board about Battelle's shortcomings, and Edelman himself shared those concerns. In August 2002, some VNS staff went so far as to leak information to *The Washington Post* about the situation, saying that Battelle was "seriously behind in the computer programming effort for the new system" and that many of the technical people were "starting to get nervous about what they will have on election night."[5] But the executive director, Ted Savaglio, continued to reassure the networks that "we fully expect to have in place and tested a new and improved computer system that will provide to our clients what is necessary to report fully and successfully on the election in November."[6] It wasn't until late October that Savaglio warned the consortium members about serious problems with the system. The Saturday before the election, he finally admitted what knowledgeable observers had known all along, that VNS could not guarantee its system would be up and running. It might work, or it might not. "The reality is that we are not really going to know until we start processing the data and start reviewing it," he said in an interview the day before the election.[7] The subscribers hardly appreciated the timing of the announcement.

In the meantime, Tom Hannon of CNN had hired Warren Mitofsky and Joe Lenski, the co-directors of the CNN/CBS joint decision team in 2000, to prepare a limited exit poll operation and a vote-counting system to double-check on VNS. One of the recommendations made by the three journalism experts who reviewed CNN's performance on Election Night 2000 was to have more than one source of information. Given the massive expense of operating just one system—the reason the networks agreed to pool their resources in the first place— paying for a complete duplicate of the service provided by VNS was not a realistic option. But CNN was willing to pay for a limited backup system in what appeared to be the most competitive races, and it offered to include CBS in the venture, though CBS declined. The backup system worked like a charm. With the complete breakdown of Battelle's computer system for VNS, only CNN had any exit poll data on the air during Election Night 2002.

Given the posturing of the networks in 2000 about finding a replacement for VNS if it didn't improve, one might have thought that the dissolution of VNS would have prompted each of the networks either to start its own operation or find some new group to run one. But only CBS and CNN had any specific proposals. Indeed, the choices for the networks turned out to be decidedly constrained. There was barely a year until the Iowa caucuses, followed by a series of primaries and then the general election. The networks needed to turn to some experts quickly, if a new system was to be installed in time. CNN's proposal was to have Mitofsky and Lenski expand their limited backup operation for CNN in 2002 to become the full-fledged operation for the consortium in 2004. The competing CBS proposal called for the operation to be under the direct control of that network, though it would hire many of the former VNS employees, including those paid for by the other networks. But the other networks didn't like the idea of being subservient to CBS.[8] And besides, that was essentially the old system that had failed, while Lenski and Mitofsky had shown they could put a new system together that worked.

The two pollsters prepared a proposal that would have the networks subscribe to the election night service provided by Edison Media Research, the company Lenski helped found, and Mitofsky International. The networks would have certain rights over the design of the questionnaire and related editorial details, but Edison/Mitofsky would be responsible for all of the technical details. No longer would the networks be able to micromanage the operation. If the system failed, it would indeed be the fault of Edison/Mitofsky, not the networks.

There were some reservations, as *The Washington Post* noted, about dealing with Mitofsky's "formidable" personality, but time was short.[9] The networks accepted the proposal. Within nine months, the new operation, the National Election Poll (NEP) was up and running, in time to test its capabilities for California's recall election on October 7, 2003, when Arnold Schwarzenegger defeated Governor Gray Davis. A month later, Edison/Mitofsky also collected election night data for the gubernatorial races in Mississippi and Kentucky. Except for minor adjustments, the system was ready for prime time. From the Iowa caucuses on January 19 through the primaries on March 9, 2004, Edison/Mitofsky projected winners in twenty-three Democratic primaries and caucuses with no errors. Now, on Election Night 2004, the system would undergo its most strenuous test yet—collecting, processing, and distributing data for races in all fifty states and Washington, D.C.

MITOFSKY'S PREDICTION OF the next day's headlines as I arrived at Edison/Mitofsky headquarters suggested he believed the preliminary exit poll data to be accurate. Only four days before, on October 29, the

Arab television station Al Jazeera had broadcast a videotape of Osama bin Laden threatening new attacks on the United States. Political analysts were divided in what effect bin Laden's sudden reappearance might have on the election. Some thought it might help Bush by reminding voters the country was at war, reinforcing a major theme of the Bush campaign. Others thought it could help Kerry by reminding the public that the Bush administration had been unable to capture the mastermind of the 9/11 terrorist attacks on the United States.[10] Most final pre-election polls showed Bush edging Kerry by a couple of percentage points, but the early results of the exit polls showed Kerry up by three percentage points. Thus it seemed that Mitofsky might be right: bin Laden helps Kerry.

At that time in the afternoon, just one of three waves of data had been entered into the computer, but a second wave was imminent. An hour and a half later, after a careful examination of the updated results, Mitofsky's confidence in the early results was shaken. He and Lenski initiated a conference call with the NEP decision teams to warn them about possibly erroneous data. The exit polls showed much larger margins for Kerry in seven states and larger margins for Bush in two states than what was expected. I asked Mitofsky why he felt the data were wrong in those states. "The priors [pre-election polls] are so different from the exit polls, it raises a red flag," he said.

Though the NEP members were warned about a likely bias in the exit polls, mostly favoring Kerry, that warning was not shared with the several other media organizations that were not NEP members but subscribed to the service. (Later, Lenski and Mitofsky would apologize for the oversight and promise to rectify that process in future elections.) Nor, of course, was the warning shared with the Internet bloggers, who were not able to subscribe to the consortium service but seemed to know the exit poll results almost as soon as they were posted. The information was supposed to be proprietary and not shared with any but the NEP members and the media subscribers, but many reporters routinely exchange such information with politicians and bloggers despite the many enjoiners not to do so. Thus, by late afternoon, the journalistic-political community was abuzz with the surprising exit poll results, showing Kerry leading Bush by substantial margins in states that were close, and showing tight races in states where Bush was expected to win. Nationally, an early estimate showed Kerry winning the popular vote by 51 percent to 48 percent, a close but clear victory.

Television reporters had been warned against sharing the results with viewers, or more subtly characterizing the race as positive or negative for any candidate. But many anchors could not help themselves, and an astute observer could quickly infer that Kerry was doing well. And if the anchors were too subtle, there were always the politicians, also the illegal recipients of the exit poll data. Typical of the kind of comments on television were those of Senator Ted Kennedy about 7:15 P.M. ET, responding to the anchor's questions about the toughness of the campaign. After giving his views, he declined further comment, indicating he didn't want to be the center of attention, because "this is John Kerry's night." It was written all over his face: Kerry would be the next president of the United States.

To its credit, Edison/Mitofsky refused to call several states where the exit polls indicated Kerry was the sure winner, because of discrepancies between the exit polls and the pre-election polls. The pollsters waited to make these calls later in the evening, when actual vote counts could supplement the results. But the decidedly Democratic bias in the exit polls also delayed calls in states that Bush would eventually win by substantial margins. The lack of early calls in such states spurred some reporters to suggest that Bush must not be faring as well in the election as had been expected.

★

7:00 P.M. ET: Among the six states whose polls have just closed, Edison/Mitofsky call Bush the winner in Kentucky, Georgia, and Tennessee; Kerry the winner in Vermont. No call is made for either South Carolina or Virginia. Some political observers think South Carolina's Senator John Edwards might persuade the state to support the Kerry-Edwards ticket, but there has never been any expectation that Virginia would be competitive. Some reporters express surprise that the networks find the Virginia race too close to call. This does not augur well for Bush. (Edison/Mitofsky show Kerry up by half a percentage point.)

7:30 P.M. ET: The polls close in West Virginia, Ohio, and North Carolina, but Edison/Mitofsky project Bush the winner only in West Virginia. Ohio is expected to be competitive, but Bush certainly should win easily in North Carolina. Another red flag for the Bush campaign.

7:38 P.M. ET: The updated crosstabs are now available, showing the vote by demographic subgroups, such as gender, age, income, and party. Kerry is still ahead of Bush by 51 percent to 48 percent nationally.

7:52 P.M. ET: The CNN decision desk leader, Clyde Tucker, calls to ask for further clarification as to why Edison/Mitofsky did not call the Senate race in Oklahoma. The Republican candidate is up by 12.9 percentage points.

Again, it's the "priors," Mitofsky tells me. He doesn't trust the exit polls. Nothing's to be gained by calling the race this early, when the exit polls are so different from the pre-election polls. Need to wait for actual vote count.

8:00 P.M. ET: Polls close in sixteen states—eight are called for Kerry, three for Bush. No surprises here. But among the five states not being called is Mississippi, another state where Bush was favored overwhelmingly. It's a real shocker that the race is too close to call in this solidly Republican state. (In fact, Bush leads by 9.6 percentage points, according to the exit polls, but the small number of respondents means there is still a reasonable possibility the margin could decline.)

As a long-time resident of New Hampshire, I am astounded to see the exit polls showing Kerry ahead of Bush in that state by 15.8 percentage points and the Democratic gubernatorial candidate leading the Republican candidate by 15.1 percentage points. New Hampshire is predominantly a Republican state. Democrats can occasionally eke out small victories, but for any Democrat to win by double digits would shake up the political establishment there. I shake my head. "I don't believe it," I tell Mitofsky. He doesn't either, which is why he won't call the races there. "In New Hampshire, we've seen tremendous errors in the exit polls," he says, referring to other election years. So, he will wait for the actual vote count. And now he is worried about the same thing in Pennsylvania, a state that was supposed to be highly competitive but currently shows Kerry up by 13.5 percentage points.

8:29 P.M. ET:	South Carolina goes to Bush.
8:30 P.M. ET:	Polls close in Arkansas, but no call for Bush.
8:35 P.M. ET:	North Carolina goes to Bush.
8:39 P.M. ET:	Virginia goes to Bush.
8:47 P.M. ET:	Mitofsky is looking at a computer screen showing the vote count compared with the exit polls: "So the exit polls did suck," he says, and shakes his head. He is not pleased.
8:48 P.M. ET:	Much has changed since the expectation of a Kerry victory earlier in the evening. Now the political commentators sense a much closer race. On television, Robert Novak notes that Bush could lose Ohio but is looking good in Florida. That leaves it up to Wisconsin and Iowa.
9:00 P.M. ET:	Polls close in fifteen states, but only eight are called—six for Bush, two for Kerry. The surprise is the no-call for Louisiana, which should be a sure state for Bush.

9:05 P.M. ET: Mark Schulman, the ABC contact person, is mystified. "The exit polls have had a large Democratic bias," he says. "I wonder why?" I repeat what I have heard from Mitofsky and Lenski: Maybe Democrats are more intense about their candidate and more likely to respond to the exit poll interviewers? "Maybe," he says. But this amount of bias is unprecedented.

9:26 P.M. ET: Louisiana to Bush.

9:28 P.M. ET: Mississippi to Bush.

BY TEN O'CLOCK it had become clear that a Kerry victory was not a certainty after all, that the exit polls were wrong in many states, and the national exit poll results were clearly off the mark. The presidential race was turning out to be as competitive as the pre-election polls had indicated. On NBC, Tim Russert outlined several paths to victory for the candidates, taking into account the states that had not yet been called. "George Bush has two or three paths to 270," Russert said, alluding to the number of electoral votes needed to win. "John Kerry has one, and it goes through Ohio."[11]

But the contest in Ohio was much too close to call. While the computer projections showed Kerry ahead by about three percentage points, the statistical analysis suggested the projection was not a certainty and should not be made. Moreover, there was a completely new problem in Ohio that would complicate any attempt to project the winner in that state.

Prior to the election, both the Bush and Kerry campaigns had, in the words of a long-time political journalist with the *Columbus Dispatch*, "scared up every ambulatory person in the state to go out and vote," resulting in such a "massive registration" that the new voters overwhelmed the poll workers on election night.[12] Some of the lists that poll workers had were not updated or not completely accurate with all appropriate information, and many potential voters were told they were not authorized to vote. In such cases, the voters were allowed to fill out provisional ballots, to be counted later if it could be determined that the potential voter had in fact registered in that precinct as required by law. The problem for projection was that no one knew how many provisional ballots there were. Moreover, it wasn't clear how the provisional ballots would break for the two candidates, though the conventional wisdom was—given the kinds of problems being reported in Ohio in mostly Democratic precincts—that Kerry would get the lion's share.[13]

Given that expected bias in favor of Kerry, the provisional ballots would not have been a problem for projection had Kerry's lead persisted throughout the night. But as I watched the Ohio figures in the latter part of the evening, Kerry's lead gradually disappeared and then eventually morphed into a small Bush lead.

9:37 P.M. ET:	3.4 percent Kerry lead
9:57 P.M. ET:	2.1 percent Kerry lead
10:11 P.M. ET:	0.3 percent Kerry lead
10:19 P.M. ET:	0.1 percent Kerry lead
10:27 P.M. ET	0.6 percent Kerry lead
10:46 P.M. ET:	0.0 percent—even
00:07 P.M. ET:	2.9 percent Bush lead
00:41 P.M. ET:	Fox calls Ohio for Bush
00:49 P.M. ET:	2.4 percent Bush lead
00:59 P.M. ET:	NBC calls Ohio for Bush
1:27 P.M. ET:	2.3 percent Bush lead

When Fox projected Bush the winner in Ohio at 12:41 in the morning, that gave him 269 electoral votes, according to that network. NBC's call for Bush eighteen minutes later also gave the president 269 electoral votes, just one short of what he needed to win. None of the other networks, nor Edison/Mitofsky, called Ohio at that time, and in fact none of them would call Ohio until Kerry eventually conceded late Wednesday morning. The problem was the provisional ballots. That night, estimates of the number of such ballots ranged from about 130,000 to 250,000. Given the number of estimated outstanding votes, plus the possibility of such a large number of provisional ballots going for Kerry, no one could tell for certain whether Kerry could catch up. Sheldon Gawiser, NBC's director of elections, later told me that he had taken the provisional ballots into account before calling Ohio for Bush. Gawiser said he used a "matrix analysis" to assess whether Kerry could overcome the deficit, and concluded he couldn't, unless he won virtually all of the provisional ballots. Gawiser did not say how many provisional ballots he assumed there were, but he must have assumed the lower rather than the higher range of estimates. Bush's lead at the time of NBC's call was about 120,000 voteswith up to the same amount outstanding, plus the provisional ballots.[14] If the latter came close to 250,000, and Kerry had taken 75 percent of them—not the extreme 100 percent scenario Gawiser suggested, and not necessarily a wild assumption about the proportion of provisional ballots that would go to the Democratic candidate—Kerry would have won. But Fox and NBC were lucky. Ultimately, it turned out there were only about 125,000 officially valid provisional ballots, and Bush ended up officially with close to a 119,000-vote margin. Still, "they shouldn't have called Ohio," Mitofsky said. "It was irresponsible. Why would you stick your neck out like that? Didn't they learn anything in 2000?"[15]

NOW THAT THE two networks had Bush at 269 electoral votes, they were in a position to project him the overall winner, once he won another state. At 2:53 in the morning, the Associated Press projected Bush the winner in Nevada, the first to do so. Edison/Mitofsky held off, saying the lead was too small and too many votes were outstanding to make that a safe call. But less than an hour later, Edison/Mitofsky also called Nevada. Within half an hour, all the networks but Fox and NBC had Bush winning that state. At the Edison/Mitofsky headquarters, at 4:30 in the morning, about fifteen or twenty bleary-eyed analysts, statisticians, and associates were milling about in front of the bank of televisions, laughing and joking as NBC and Fox held fast to not calling Nevada. If either did so, as all the other decision teams had done, it would have been the first to project Bush the overall winner. But NBC had been the first to miscall Florida for Gore, and later Fox had been the first to miscall Florida for Bush. Neither apparently wanted to risk being the scapegoat again. "It's reverse chicken," Mitofsky said. "They're daring each other *not* to call the race." *The Chicago Sun Times* later headlined, "For hours we knew what they wouldn't say."[16]

The decision teams at both NBC and Fox denied they were chicken to call Nevada for fear of being first to call Bush the winner.[17] Each claimed it was the outstanding votes in that state that deterred them. But NBC News Vice President Bill Wheatley seemed to contradict the NBC decision team when he suggested he would not have been "entirely comfortable" calling Nevada because that would have made NBC the only network to project Bush the overall winner.[18] And NBC anchor Tom Brokaw was more explicit, saying on the *Today* show the next morning that the network did not call any more states after bringing Bush to 269 electoral votes with Ohio, in order to avoid making "a judgment about who the president-elect is."[19]

Media Furor and Conspiracies Galore

Despite differences of opinion about the Ohio and Nevada projections, the networks acquitted themselves well in election 2000. And Lenski and Mitofsky could reasonably claim that they had done a good job, in a very constricted period of time, to give the networks the election data they needed. Although many of the state exit polls were far off the mark, Mitofsky and Lenski had recognized that possibility, warned the consortium members, and held off making projections until they received the actual vote count. Some of the calls for Bush were later than they would have been had the exit polls been accurate. South Carolina, Virginia, Mississippi, North Carolina, Arkansas, Arizona, and Louisiana all ended up in the Bush column, as expected, with Bush's margin of victory at least eight percentage points. Accurate exit polls would probably have been sufficient information for Edison/Mitofsky to call each of these states at their respective poll-closing times. But the fact is that all the states were eventually called accurately; Edison/Mitofsky made no miscalls during the election, and neither did any of the networks.

If they did such a good job, why all the post-election furor about the exit polls? *Washington Post* managing editor Steven Coll said of the exit poll data received by his newspaper, "We think it wasn't worth what we paid for it, that's for sure."[20] Bill Keller, the executive editor of *The New York Times*, wrote a letter to the consortium asking for a partial refund of the fee paid by his newspaper, because he felt they had been "ill-served" by the data.[21] A similar complaint came from Don Frederick, national political editor of the *Los Angeles Times*, who did not ask for a refund but promised to review whether the paper should ever subscribe to the service again.[22] The major complaint of the newspapers was that the exit polls misled them in the preparation of stories on the election, causing them to focus on what would happen in the country with a new Kerry administration rather than on the implications of a second term for Bush. With deadlines approaching, the newspapers suddenly had to produce new stories to take into account the change in poll numbers.

Part of the problem was a computer glitch. At a little before eleven in the evening Eastern Time, Edison/Mitofsky intended to post the new weighted numbers showing Bush in the lead nationally, which could have provided more accurate information to the newspapers. But suddenly the computer screens froze. Later Lenski explained that it wasn't the whole analytical system that failed; in fact, from time to time the screens would come back up with the latest county data. The problem occurred because of the message log. Throughout the evening, Lenski and Mitofsky would send notes to the subscribers about the forthcoming results, but the computer program did not make enough room to archive all of the messages. That very minor part of the over-all projection system resulted in intermittent frozen screens, and an inability to update the national figures. Not until after one in the morning was the whole system transferred to a backup server and all the national and state numbers updated.[23]

But a larger problem was that the overall national exit poll, and many of the state exit polls, were just plain wrong. By wrong I mean they either indicated the wrong winner, as was the case with the national exit poll showing Kerry in the lead, or they were so far off the actual results they misled the poll users about the true character of the contest in the states. The television networks may have been ultimately well served by the exit poll operation, but the newspapers with their relatively early deadlines to publish were less fortunate.

Apart from some subscribers' dissatisfaction with the flawed exit polls there was an even larger problem—the proliferation of conspiracy theories to explain the discrepancies between the exit polls and the vote count. "The erroneous results are keeping the Internet abuzz with suggestions that something was awry in the November 2 presidential election," wrote Julia Malone for the Cox News Service. "Theorists on the left have alleged that the variation between early exit polls and the election result means that the vote count must be wrong. Internet post-ings from the right counter that the exit polls were designed with a pro-Kerry tilt and then publicized in an attempt to discourage President Bush's supporters from going to the polls."[24]

One of the staunchest advocates of the exit-polls-are-right, the-vote-counts-are-wrong theory was Steven Freeman, a statistician and visit-ing professor at the University of Pennsylvania, who posted a critique on the Web shortly after the election. In it he argued that exit polls are typ-ically very accurate measures of voter intent, and that the discrepancies between the exit polls and the actual vote count in the country overall, and especially in the most competitive states, "could not have been due to chance or random error."[25] He was supported in his views by two other experts, who also posted a paper shortly after the election asserting that the "substantial discrepancy . . . between the national exit poll and the popular vote count" was not caused by random error or by a "skewed exit poll," but was most likely explained by "widespread breakdown of the voting process and accuracy of the vote count."[26]

They all disagreed with Lenski and Mitofsky, who said that the mostly Democratic bias in the exit poll results was due primarily to the fact that disproportionately more Democrats were willing to be interviewed than were Republicans. In their after-action report, the two pollsters presented findings to show that the Democratic bias in their polls was not because they had chosen the wrong sample precincts. The *actual vote count* in their samples represented the overall results very closely. But the *poll results* in those same precincts differed from the vote count by an average error of 6.5 percentage points (favoring Kerry) in the Kerry-Bush difference, the largest bias in the past five elections. In practical terms, that meant on average if a precinct's final vote tally showed Bush and Kerry tied, the poll in that precinct would have shown Kerry winning by 6.5 percentage points. By contrast, the average Democratic bias in 2000 was just 1.8 percentage points, in 1988 and 1996 it was 2.2 points, and in 1992 it was 5.0 points.[27]

The tendency of one group of voters to decline to participate in polls more than another group is referred to as "non-response bias," and there is no sure way to correct for it. When people refuse to participate in the exit poll, analysts cannot know if those people happen to be conservative or liberal, or Republican or Democrat. But if Republicans are more skeptical about the exit polls and the mainstream media, and thus more likely not to participate; or if Democrats are more eager than Republicans to report their vote choice, and therefore agree to participate more often than Republicans, the poll results in that precinct would be biased in favor of Kerry. And that, according to Mitofsky and Lenski, is exactly what happened. "There were certainly motivational factors that are impossible to quantify, but which led to Kerry voters being less likely than Bush voters to refuse to take the survey," they write. "In addition there are interactions between respondents and interviewers that can contribute to differential non-response rates."[28]

Those interaction factors include how far the interviewers had to stand away from the voting area, the size of the precincts, and the weather. The greater the distance, the larger the precincts, and the worse the weather, the greater the poll error. Also, younger interviewers produced larger poll errors than older interviewers, suggesting experience was an important element in how well the interviewers performed their duties. However, these interviewer factors played a relatively minor role in the poll error. Even the most favorable circumstances produced significant discrepancies between the exit polls and the actual vote. Thus, the key to the polling errors was not the characteristics of the interviewers and the conditions during the election, but rather the motivation of the voters—their personal decisions about whether to participate in the exit poll or not.

Freeman and others disagreed with these conclusions and on January 31, 2005, they posted an article on USCountVotes.org that outlined their objections.[29] In April, they posted another more detailed analysis,[30] though one of the group's endorsers was no longer on the list. That person was Elizabeth Liddle, a fifty-something mother and University of Nottingham graduate student who had reevaluated her position after developing a computational model that undermined the USCountVotes objections to the Mitofsky-Lenski report. At the annual meeting of the American Association for Public Opinion Research in May 2005 at Miami Beach, Mitofsky presented findings that confirmed her model. Also at the conference, one of the authors of the USCountVotes paper, Ron Baiman, presented another paper that claimed to refute Liddle's work. His credibility was reduced, however, since only four of the original twelve author-endorsers of the USCountVotes report signed on to this new paper.[31]

The debate seemed like it would never end. But then one of the twelve original USCountVote authors, Bruce O'Dell, vice president and co-founder of U.S. Count Votes, posted his own research contradicting Baiman's conclusions. O'Dell wrote that when he applied the "Liddle bias index" to his own computer simulations, the results contradicted the central thesis of the Baiman paper, and of the argument that he himself had previously accepted. He was now persuaded that the discrepancies between the vote count and the exit polls did not, by themselves, prove vote fraud. Like Liddle, he does not argue that vote fraud did not occur in the 2004 election, only that the erroneous exit polls do not provide convincing evidence for such fraud.[32]

The conspiracy theories on the right were not directly addressed in that debate among the statistical experts, but the distrust in exit polls expressed by the two groups was similar. And the evidence that exit polls were indeed wrong, most likely because of nonresponse bias, undermined the notion that the exit poll results were deliberately manipulated to depress Republican voter turnout. That was the argument made by columnist Dick Morris,[33] a conservative Republican (who was also an advisor to former President Bill Clinton), and his ideological companion, John Wambaugh.[34] Supposedly, all of the networks and Edison/Mitofsky were in on a scheme to make it appear early in the evening that Kerry was going to win, thus causing some Republican voters in western states not to vote because there was no chance their candidate would win. The argument never seemed to have any legs anyway, and it died in relative obscurity, perhaps because it would have required a degree of cooperation unheard of among the different news organizations. Also, the net result of the bad polls was at worst some veiled comments on television that Bush was not doing as well as expected, hardly worth all of the effort at deception in the first place—especially since it has never been shown that such comments either stimulate or depress voter turnout. Still, the fact that the exit polls genuinely "sucked," as Mitofsky so elegantly put it, should have brought a big sigh of relief to Morris, Wambaugh, and their readers, reassured now that some leftwing nuts had not infiltrated and manipulated the exit polls for their own nefarious ends.

PERHAPS THE PEOPLE who were angriest with Edison/Mitofsky were the bloggers who spread the early results of the exit polls as though they were truth incarnate. "The false picture had real impact," wrote Rich Morin of *The Washington Post*. "The stock market plummeted nearly 100 points in the last two hours of trading, and the evening news was replete with veiled hints of good news to come for the Kerry campaign."[35] But Mitofsky and Lenski reacted with anger themselves. "The early release came from unauthorized leaks to bloggers who posted misinformation," Mitofsky emailed to Keith Olbermann of *Countdown*. "The leakers were reading complex displays intended for trained statisticians. The leakers did not understand what they were reading and the bloggers did not know they were getting misinformation." While "all the professionals correctly interpreted the numbers," he continued, "only the unauthorized leakers and bloggers were misled—a fate they richly deserve."[36]

Lenski was no less strident. "I'm not designing polls for some blogger who doesn't even understand how to read the data," he told the *Los Angeles Times*.[37]

Jack Shafer of *Slate*, one of the several Web sites that posted exit poll data without a legal right to do so, disagreed with Mitofsky's partner. "It is Lenski and the networks who are at fault for not telling viewers—and bloggers—the deeper meaning of exit poll data."[38]

A response by a fellow pollster on the AAPOR membership net found Shafer's response amusing. "Here Shafer overlooks the fact that his organization and drudgereport.com, wonkette.com, dailykos.com, mydd.com are STEALING. They didn't pay for the information they posted so freely. This is something like a thief blaming the car owner for not providing the operating manual."[39]

One reporter saw a positive aspect to the brouhaha caused by the erroneous exit poll results. "The resulting furor was the best thing that could have happened to journalism, to polling, and to the bloggers who made this year's Election Day such a cheap thrill. That's because the 2004 election may have finally stripped exit polling of its reputation as the crown jewel of political surveys."[40] Or, as CNN's political commentator Bill Schneider noted, "The lesson here is—put not your faith in exit polls."[41]

Our lengthy and critical self-examination shows that we
let our viewers down. I apologize for making those bad
projections that night. It will not happen again.

—*Roger Ailes, chairman and CEO, Fox News Network, February 14, 2001*

We are embarrassed by those errors. . . .
We are absolutely intent on avoiding them and
making sure they don't happen again.

—*Andrew Lack, president, NBC News, February 14, 2001*

We did make a mistake that night. You got us. And I think
we are here not only to assure you that we will fix it,
but it won't happen again.

—*Tom Johnson, chairman and CEO, CNN, February 14, 2001*

So we have a tremendous incentive . . . not to let this
ever happen again.

—*Andrew Heyward, President, CBS News, February 14, 2001*

These mistakes cannot be allowed to happen again.

—*Louis D. Baccardi, president and CEO, Associated Press, February 14, 2001*

Nothing can keep the networks from someday calling
another race incorrectly.

—*Warren Mitofsky, March 3, 2004*

9

Never Say Never Again

Whenever a major catastrophe occurs, there are always people who will call for steps to avoid such a disaster in the future. That certainly was the prevailing sentiment during the congressional hearings on February 14, 2001, when almost every person who spoke before the committee either explicitly stated or at least implied that what happened on Election Night 2000 should never happen again. The review committee that evaluated CNN's performance on election night expressed the same sentiment, arguing that in the future "a state should not be said to have gone for a particular candidate until enough votes have been counted to make the outcome in that state a *certainty*."[1]

The networks adopted many changes to avoid the specific problems of Election 2000, but even if the changes all work, that doesn't mean there will be no more erroneous calls, or that such miscalls won't have significant consequences for the political environment. Nor does it suggest there won't be new problems, unforeseen, but with as significant an impact as the Florida miscalls in 2000. The problems in 2004, with the early results of exit polls bandied about the Internet, illustrate how easy it is to correct old problems only to have new ones come to the fore. Still, it's worthwhile noting that many of the reforms suggested by the special Research Triangle Institute review of Voter News Service were adopted by Edison/Mitofsky. Had the reforms been in effect in 2000, all four miscalls—the two in Florida, the presidential race in New Mexico, and the U.S. Senate race in Washington—would not have been made.

When Mitofsky and Lenski took over the election night projection system, they converted it from DOS-based software to Windows software, which allows analysts greater and easier access to more information. One of the key problems in 2000 was the comparison of the presidential voting patterns that night with just the 1998 gubernatorial election, when the 1996 presidential election was a more appropriate basis of comparison. The computer system in 2000 actually had the results of both earlier statewide elections available for comparison, but the software limitations forced a choice between showing the comparisons for either the 1998 or the 1996 elections, but not both. In the new system, the analysts can view the comparison of current election results with three previous elections. Had the analysts been able to see the discrepancy between the projections based on the 1996 election and the projections based on the 1998 election, Mitofsky says, they would probably not have projected Gore the winner in Florida.[2]

The new software also provides more quality-control checks, so that any major changes in the data will immediately be flagged for review. Had this system been in effect in 2000, it is likely—though not certain—that the 20,000-vote erroneous entry in Volusia County at 2:08 in the morning would have been detected and questions asked before the networks called the election for Bush.

The Edison/Mitofsky system has also made an adjustment to the calculation of the precinct sampling error, which gives an incorrect reading when it is based on partial, rather than complete, vote counts. Had the adjustment of the statistic been in place in 2000, there probably would not have been the "screenful of Gore" about eight o'clock in the evening that John Ellis described to his cousins—and thus no projection of the vice president as the winner in Florida.

The Edison/Mitofsky operation has also adopted the "1 percent" rule, the only reform that would have definitely prevented the networks from calling Florida for Bush. If calculations of the outstanding vote show that a candidate will probably win, but with a margin of less than 1 percent of the overall vote, no projection will be made. This rule is essentially an outgrowth of Murray Edelman's memo to all VNS subscribers just before the 2000 election about the potential size of data errors. The memo related that in past elections there had been errors in the vote count as large as .54 percent—just over one half of 1 percent—of the total vote. By instituting the 1 percent rule, Edison/Mitofsky have expanded the warning to allow for a larger error in the data. At 2:15 in the morning of Election Night 2000, the CNN/CBS decision team projected Bush to win Florida with a margin of just over 30,000 votes, only one half of 1 percent of the six million expected votes. At 2:40 in the morning, the projected margin was just over 40,000 votes—about two thirds of 1 percent. At no time did it appear that Bush would win with as much as a 60,000 vote—or 1 percent—margin. Had the 1 percent rule been in effect for all the networks, they would not have projected Bush the winner.

Two of the networks—ABC and NBC—have adopted a policy of insulating their decision teams from news coverage, so in theory the teams don't know what calls the other networks are making. Sheldon Gawiser of NBC assured me that when he and his decision team projected John Kerry the winner in Ohio at 12:59 in the morning after Election Day 2004, eighteen minutes after Fox had already made the same projection, he had no idea whether any other network had made the call. Unlike 2000, the NBC call could not have been influenced by the fact that Fox called Ohio first. Still, CBS, Fox, and CNN have all rejected insulating their decision teams. And CBS has gone in the other direction, putting its decision team in the newsroom, so that information is available to the team members from reporters and other news sources.

★

WHILE SOME OF these changes may help to address the problems in previous years, the problems with election night projections in the future, Gawiser believes, will probably not be the same as they have been. New problems will surface with the increasingly complex models that are needed to incorporate the rise in absentee and early voting, and even all-mail voting, adopted by the states. In 2004, absentee and early voting accounted for more than 30 percent of the vote in eleven states, and from 20 to 30 percent of the vote in seven other states.[3] To take into account all the voters who could not be reached by the exit polls on Election Day, Edison/Mitofsky conducted special pre-election telephone polls in thirteen states,[4] and the number is likely to rise as more states encourage absentee and early voting. Such surveys are very expensive because of the difficulty in getting hold of actual voters. If 20 percent of all voters in the state are absentee, and the statewide turnout is about 50 percent, that means only about one in ten households the interviewer reaches is likely to have a voter. And on average these days, interviewers have to call five households to get one respondent. If the absentee vote constitutes one fifth of the voters, that would mean fifty households have to be called to get one absentee voter.

More important, the pre-election polls of absentee and early voters do not provide as useful data for projections as would be obtained from voters in an exit poll. The computer projection models are based on obtaining precinct and county data, which can then be compared with past voting patterns. The pre-election poll results cannot be integrated into those models.

Probably the biggest impact of early and absentee voting is on the projection of close races. It can be difficult getting accurate information from the counties about the number of absentee and early votes that have yet to be counted, adding yet another potential source of error to the models. According to Edelman, each state has a different way of handling the absentee votes. In some states, they are all counted at one time; in others, they are counted in stages. As VNS editorial director, he could never be sure when all the absentee votes were actually included in the vote count. In election 2000, for example, four of the networks (all but Fox) had called New Mexico for Gore by 10:30 P.M. ET; and VNS called it by 3:00 the next morning. The polls closed in that state at 9:00 P.M., and by the time the networks made the projection, the votes in nearly half the precincts had been counted.[5] Bernalillo County, the state's largest, had reported that all but 2,000 of its early and absentee votes had also been counted. But there were software problems that led officials to remove 67,000 of these votes for a recount shortly after the VNS call in the morning. Gore eventually won by less than 400 votes. The race should never have been called, but the data error was caused by problems in Bernalillo County, not by VNS or the networks.

ANOTHER MAJOR AND persistent problem with the exit polls is a partisan bias that tends to favor Democrats, but also sometimes favors Republicans. If the bias were consistently large and in always in favor of the Democrats, a statistical adjustment could be made to correct for the problem. But the bias is not predictable either in magnitude or direction, and there's not much that the pollsters can do to correct for it. Edison/Mitofsky can do a better job of training the interviewers to reduce the problem, but most of the bias stems from the fact that about half of all voters who are asked to participate in the exit poll simply refuse. More often Republicans refuse at a higher rate than Democrats, but in some precincts, it's the other way around. This differential refusal means that the resulting sample of voters in the precinct consists of either too many Democrats or too many Republicans. In 2004, the Democratic bias was much greater than the Republican bias, which explained why the exit polls showed Kerry winning nationally by three percentage points, and in several states by margins that were much larger than those resulting from the final vote count.

Still, even when the exit polls are biased in favor of one party or the other, that doesn't necessarily mean the exit polls lead to erroneous projections. When results appear too far off in comparison with "priors" (pre-election polls) or the state's voting history, the computer models will note the problems and analysts will wait for actual vote counts to check on whether the exit poll data can be used. That is what happened in 2004, when late in the afternoon, long before the networks would be considering projecting winners, Edison/Mitofsky sent out a message to its subscribers warning them of the bias. And in the states where the bias appeared most pronounced, all the decision teams waited for actual vote returns before projecting any candidate a winner. The problems caused by the bias came not from miscalls but from bloggers who spread the word of a Kerry victory long before the data justified such a conclusion. Starting in 2006, Edison/Mitofsky will not release any exit poll results to their subscribers until late in the afternoon Eastern Time, in order to minimize the potential damage that can occur when bloggers essentially steal preliminary exit poll results and spread them around the Internet.

A PERENNIAL ISSUE that will continue to plague election night projections, especially during presidential elections, is the "early call" effect. Both Democrats and Republicans have decried the networks for calling state winners before all the precincts in that state have closed. In the wake of the 2000 election, all the networks promised that in the future they would withhold projections in any state until the all the polls in that state are closed. And in both 2002 and 2004, they kept their collective promise. But that still means polls may be open in the West when the networks project winners in some eastern and southern states. More than 80 percent of the electoral votes come from states where the polls close by 9:00 P.M. ET, so that it is quite possible for a presidential candidate to have won the required 270 electoral votes in states where the polls have closed, while polls are still open in many of the western states. An extreme example occurred in 1980, when NBC projected Ronald Reagan the winner with 270 electoral votes by 8:15 P.M. ET, when the polls in most of the country were still open, including many of the states for which projections were made. While it was unusual to project an overall winner so soon, a presidential winner has been announced before poll closings on the West Coast in eight of the last twelve presidential elections (1960 through 2004), including seven announcements at least 100 minutes prior to those poll closings.[6]

But does it matter? Are voters discouraged, encouraged, or unaffected by vote projections showing their favored candidate or political party losing in other states? In preparing the CBS post-election report in 2000, CBS News Director of Surveys Kathleen Frankovic, a Ph.D. with numerous scholarly publications, undertook an extensive review of the academic literature on the subject of the early-call effect. "It is impossible to prove a negative," she wrote. "There is little evidence that early election calls affect turnout or voting patterns, but there is no way to prove that these calls have *no* effect on voting."[7] These sentiments are echoed by Professor William C. Adams of George Washington University, whose comprehensive review of more than twenty years of studies concluded that claims of network projections causing a decline in voter turnout have not been substantiated. "Faced with a strong body of evidence to the contrary, this particular argument against projections has collapsed."[8]

Despite the negative findings from numerous studies, or the unreliable findings from several other poor-quality studies, the public and many politicians are convinced that early calls affect voters' behavior. It's always the losers who complain, of course, so conventional wisdom is that people are discouraged from voting if they see signs that their favored party or candidates are losing.

This widespread public perception that early calls depress voter turnout for one party or the other has spurred all of the networks to support uniform poll-closing legislation. Numerous bills have been introduced into the Congress on this subject, usually setting the closing time for all polls in the country at 9:00 P.M. ET, although some have specified an hour or even two hours later. The bills typically allow Hawaii and Alaska to open their polls the day before Election Day, because the uniform closing time would force the polls to close in the afternoon in those states. The bills would also extend daylight savings time for two weeks in the West in order to allow a local closing time of 7:00 P.M.

The last time uniform poll closing bills were introduced was in 2001, when several legislators submitted different versions, including the two U.S. senators from Alaska, Ted Stevens and Frank Murkowski, and a U.S. senator from Hawaii, Daniel Inouye.[9] In the 1980s, the House twice passed a uniform poll-closing bill that would have excluded Hawaii and Alaska from its provisions, but the Senate failed to concur.[10] Despite all the bills, and despite Representative Billy Tauzin's expressed support for such legislation during the 2001 congressional hearings, no uniform poll-closing bill has been enacted into law, leaving the public and politicians beating up on the networks for the early-call effect.[11]

THE 2000 ELECTION raised once again a question that has been asked since television first began covering elections: whether the networks should even try to project winners. While each network undertook some type of investigation of what went wrong on election night, only CNN commissioned a wholly independent and outside committee to look into the matter, and only that committee, among all the networks' special investigatory committees, addressed the fundamental questions: "What were the networks doing? Why were they doing it?"

Those weren't the questions that Tom Johnson, chairman and CEO of CNN, asked his specially selected committee to address. He wanted to know: "What went wrong at CNN? Why did it happen? What should be done to guard against a recurrence in future elections?"[12] These questions assumed that the status quo was pretty much okay, but that errors had occurred that needed to be fixed. The independent committee, however, had an agenda of its own, to attack the whole premise that election night projections were a useful journalistic undertaking. Their opening preamble set the tone: "On Election Day 2000, television news organizations staged a collective drag race on the crowded highway of democracy, recklessly endangering the electoral process, the political life of the country, and their own credibility, all for reasons that may be conceptually flawed and commercially questionable."[13] While other investigatory committees, and even the independent RTI report, focused on ways to make the projections more accurate, the CNN review committee was more intent on halting the projections altogether.

The CNN review committee included three journalist-scholars with impeccable credentials and extensive journalistic experience: Joan Konner, professor and dean emerita of Columbia University Graduate School of Journalism, and an award-winning television journalist; James Risser, a two-time Pulitzer prize–winning newspaper reporter and the former director of the John S. Knight Fellowships for Professional Journalists at Stanford University; and Ben Wattenberg, moderator of PBS's weekly program *Think Tank* and a senior fellow at the American Enterprise Institute, who has authored or co-authored eight books on public opinion, politics, and social demographics. They argued that the network should not use exit polls for projections, no matter what the results showed. "Even if exit polling is made more accurate," the authors wrote, "it will never be as accurate as a properly conducted actual vote count."[14] And they went on to recommend against any announcement of winners until the vote count has essentially been completed statewide. They objected to the use of sample precincts to project winners, preferring instead that the networks wait for the vote count from all precincts. And they said that the 1-in-200 risk the networks were willing to take of being wrong was too risky. They wanted no "projection" of winners, but an announcement that a candidate has won once the election outcome is "certain." "Any statements broadcast prior to that time," they wrote, "should be limited to stating who is leading and with what percentage of the vote counted."[15]

This was a solution that was the proverbial tossing the baby out with the bathwater. They wanted the networks to go back four decades, when CBS and NBC were competing with each other in simply reporting the actual vote count. In their idealism, they ignored more than a century of efforts by the news media—first newspapers, then radio, and now television (soon to be augmented by the Internet)—to tell citizens who the winners are as quickly as possible. As CBS News Director of Surveys Kathleen Frankovic told me, "They wanted tigers to become pussycats. It'll never happen."[16]

In the past four decades, statisticians have developed sophisticated ways of analyzing vote returns, so that they can accurately project winners much faster than all the votes can be tabulated. From 1967 through 1998, Mitofsky and Edelman used the election night projection system, designed by Mitofsky and his colleagues at CBS, to make some 2,200 projections. They made only six miscalls, for an accuracy rate of 99.7 percent.[17] Thus, the problems with the election projection system weren't large. But they were significant. What was needed was some focused tinkering, some slowing down of the projection process, not a wholesale rejection of the system.

The Perfect Solution

On January 25, 2001, Mitofsky and Lenski, the co-directors of the joint CNN/CBS decision team, submitted a memo to CNN recommending changes that almost certainly would have prevented all the errors that had been made on all election nights since the networks started making projections. Here were the experts showing the way to what everyone at the congressional hearing said they wanted—a plan that would ensure (as much as anything in life can be certain, other than death and taxes) that what happened on Election Night 2000 would never happen again. Just two major steps proposed by Mitofsky and Lenski would suffice, along with a couple of minor adjustments:[18]

1. Reduce the risk that a projection will be wrong by increasing the "critical value" for making a call that is based solely on exit poll data, from 2.6 to 4.0 standard errors.
2. Refrain from making a projection in any race where the estimated margin of victory is less than 1 percent even when 100 percent of precincts are reporting.

The first change would lower the statistical probability of error in making calls based on exit polls alone from 1 in 200 to about 1 in 10,000. That is as close to "certainty" as one can reasonably achieve. The second change, if it had been the standard in 2000, would have prevented the miscalls in New Mexico and Washington, and the Bush miscall in Florida.

Mitofsky and Lenski made two additional recommendations. They noted that if the exit polls show a race that is too close to call, then the computer models should depend on vote returns to make new estimates of a winner. In that situation, they suggested, any projection of a winner should not be made until the computer models show a "call status" based on just the actual vote count (ignoring the exit poll results). Sometimes analysts make a projection when the computer models show a candidate in the less commanding "leading status." As the pollsters acknowledge, "We had felt comfortable with [the Gore] projection because we observed a 'leading status'. . . in other words, the best estimate based solely upon actual vote data in the sample precincts. If we had waited for a 'call status' in this estimator, the projection of Gore as the winner in Florida would never have been made."[19] Edison/Mitofsky will now call a race only when the computer models indicate a "call status."[20]

The other suggestion the pollsters made was to adjust the way absentee votes are estimated when past voting patterns suggest they will constitute 10 percent or more of the total vote. The adjustment includes surveys of absentee voters and a comparison of past absentee voting patterns with current results. Both adjustments have already been implemented.

The impact of these relatively minor changes would have been stunning. "By following these criteria," Mitofsky and Lenski wrote, "we would have avoided every single one of the wrong calls and near misses of the past several elections."[21]

At the same time, viewers would have hardly noticed any appreciable slowdown in the network coverage, except when reality demanded it. In 2000, for thirty-six states and Washington, D.C., application of the new criteria would have caused no change in the time when projections were made. That includes Oregon, which was not called on election night by any of the VNS members. For ten other states, projections would have been delayed by about half an hour up to almost two hours. And for four states that were called at some point on election night, the new rules would have precluded such projections, leaving Americans with the correct perception that the vote counting was so close a winner had not yet been decided.

HOW PROPOSED RULES FOR PROJECTING WINNERS WOULD HAVE CHANGED THE ACTUAL CALLS MADE BY CNN/CBS ON ELECTION NIGHT 2000*

State	Actual Time of Projection (Eastern Time)	Estimated New Time of Projection with New Criteria	Difference
Florida	7:50 P.M. (Gore)	No call	
Michigan	8:00 P.M.	8:40 P.M.	30 minutes
Pennsylvania	8:47 P.M.	9:40 P.M.	53 minutes

State	Actual Time of Projection (Eastern Time)	Estimated New Time of Projection with New Criteria	Difference
Louisiana	9:00 P.M.	10:10 P.M.	70 minutes
Ohio	9:16 P.M.	10:10 P.M.	54 minutes
Tennessee	9:16 P.M.	10:10 P.M.	54 minutes
Missouri	10:05 P.M.	10:40 P.M.	35 minutes
West Virginia	10:11 P.M.	10:40 P.M.	29 minutes
New Mexico	10:21 P.M.	No Call	
Nevada	11:20 P.M.	1:10 A.M.	110 minutes
Arizona	11:46 P.M.	12:40 A.M.	54 minutes
Arkansas	12:05 A.M.	1:10 A.M.	65 minutes
Iowa	2:04 A.M.	No call	
Florida	2:17 A.M. (Bush)	No call	
Wisconsin	6:22 A.M.	No call	
36 other states and Washington, D.C.			No change

*Based on estimates of Warren Mitofsky and Joe Lenski, decision team leaders for CNN/CBS on Election Night 2000.[22]

The Catch

The snag in this perfect solution is network competition, a factor decried by the network chiefs at the congressional hearings, who all declared they preferred accuracy over speed. But the truth is, as Frankovic explained, for journalists, competition "is in their blood. It's hard-wired in their brains!"[23]

Despite the relative caution of the networks in 2004, they were already at the top of the slippery slope of competitive pressures. Ironically, it began with the consortium's decision not to adopt the tougher standard for calling races that Lenski and Mitofsky themselves had recommended to CNN and that CNN's Tom Johnson promised to follow when he spoke at the congressional hearing in 2001. That new standard would have made the "critical" threshold for calling a race based solely on exit polls at 4.0 standard errors instead of 2.6, but Mitofsky dismissed the need for such a change. "A critical value of 4.0 is very rigid, and frankly, it is overkill," he wrote. "The other changes made in the system should be adequate to avoid trouble."[24]

Overkill it may be, but both Mitofsky and Lenski thought the new standard was worth it when they made the recommendation to CNN in the aftermath of the Election Night 2000 fiasco, arguing that it would have helped to avoid any errors on that election night as well on previous election nights. The "cost" of implementing the change, according to their report, was minimal. The new critical value would apply only to projections using exit polls, and the net result might mean a delay in calling a race by anywhere from half an hour to two hours at most. That seemed like a reasonable trade-off—a little less speed for a lot more accuracy. But once the spotlight of congressional concern moved on, the new standard was abandoned.

CBS's Kathleen Frankovic agrees that waiting for a critical value of 4.0 poses problems for the networks. In 2004, she found that waiting even for a critical value of 2.6, the historical criterion for calling a race, was problematic. At 8:00 P.M. ET, the polls closed in Mississippi, a state that everyone knew would go for Bush. The exit poll had a substantial lead for the president, but the computer showed that the critical value of 2.6 had not been reached. Statistically that meant that instead of being 99.5 percent confident of making a call (only one chance in 200 of being wrong), maybe they were only 99 percent confident (one chance in 100 of being wrong), or maybe even just 95 percent confident (one chance in 20 of being wrong). That lower statistical threshold could suggest caution, but CBS analysts had no doubt Bush would win in that state, regardless of what the critical value was. If they hadn't made the call, Frankovic said, "we would have looked stupid. In 2004, [it was obvious:] BUSH TAKES MISSISSIPPI!"[25]

Looking stupid wasn't the only concern. On air, political pundits tend to interpret calls that are delayed past poll-closing time as indicating a competitive race. As William Adams noted about the 2004 election, "During delays before calling the states, the misleading phrase 'too close to call' was often used on the air, suggesting that Bush and Kerry were locked in a tight battle in a state."[26] But a close race wasn't the reason Mississippi couldn't be called at closing time. The delay was caused by small sample sizes. In states where the winner is almost 100 percent assured, the consortium will select only a small number of sample precincts for the exit polls—about twenty or less in states like Mississippi—rather than the fifty or more that are used in more competitive states. It's a reasonable cost-cutting measure—better to put more resources into the competitive than the noncompetitive states, to gain higher levels of statistical confidence where it counts most—but it means statistically that in a "safe" state with few sample precincts, a candidate has to lead by a superlarge margin for the computer to show a "call status." Unfortunately, too many commentators don't understand this statistical problem and make the wrong interpretation. That bothers Frankovic. CBS's concern, she said, is to tell the election night story accurately. She does not buy into the argument that it's much better to err on the side of delaying projections than to make wrong ones. There has to be a balance, she argues. It's just as important to report accurately how well a candidate is doing during the evening as it is to avoid making erroneous projections.

With that philosophy, the CBS decision team decided not to wait for statistical certainty, but to rely more on their own judgment—or, more precisely, their own models. Frankovic notes that since 2000, CBS has developed its own "system" of election night projection. She does not feel free to discuss any details except to say their system takes all of the election information provided by Edison/Mitofsky and feeds it into the CBS computer models, which have the ability to make estimates in the same way that the Edison/Mitofsky models make estimates, although presumably with different criteria. In any case, at 8:03

P.M. ET, CBS projected Bush the winner in Mississippi when the Edison/Mitofsky models did not show the state in a "call status." The other networks waited for actual vote returns to make the projection, but that meant they called the race a full hour and a half later than CBS.[27] Frankovic was right, of course—Mississippi belonged to Bush, by a twenty-point margin, 60 percent to 40 percent. It's not clear that many people thought the other networks looked stupid for not calling Mississippi earlier, but at least people couldn't think that about CBS. A similar situation must have occurred in Montana, another safe state for Bush, which he also won by twenty points, 59 percent to 39 percent. Only CBS called it at closing time. ABC called it seventeen minutes later, Fox an hour and twenty-two minutes later, and CNN and NBC more than two hours later. Three of the networks must have waited for actual vote returns to verify the prediction, while ABC and CBS called the state based on exit polls.

When the networks call races at times that are this far apart, it indicates that some networks are willing to accept a significantly higher risk of being wrong than others. An argument could be made that the risk of calling Mississippi and Montana at closing time was minimal, that those calls were ultimately justified by the lopsided results in favor of Bush. But a similar situation occurred in Colorado, whose polls closed at 11:00 P.M. ET. Again, only CBS projected Bush the winner at that time, while the other four networks all made the same projection within a six-minute period starting at 11:20 P.M. ET, an hour and twenty minutes after the CBS call. All five networks had the same data—the Edison/Mitofsky exit poll in that state, along with the results of an Edison/Mitofsky poll of absentee voters. That CBS called the race on the basis of the exit poll and absentee voter poll, while the other networks did not, means that CBS was accepting a higher risk than the other networks of being wrong. The final results showed Bush winning by just five percentage points, 52 percent to 47 percent—a far cry from sure victory like the ones in Mississippi and Montana.

These examples do not mean that CBS typically accepts higher risk in calling races than the other networks. CBS was either the last or second-to-last network to project a winner in New Hampshire, for example. Fox projected Kerry the winner there at 12:35 A.M. ET, CNN at 1:17 A.M. ET, while CBS waited until 2:04 A.M. ET, one hour and thirty-nine minutes later than Fox, and forty-seven minutes later than CNN. Kerry won the state with just a one-point margin, 50 percent to 49 percent. In this case, Fox and CNN were willing to accept higher risks than CBS, which waited until more votes had been counted before making the call. The very small margin would seem to have demanded special caution, which CBS clearly gave. Also, later on Election Night 2004, only NBC and Fox—not CBS, ABC, nor CNN—called Ohio, a projection that Mitofsky characterized as "irresponsible." That call had different kinds of risks, because of uncertain information about the provisional ballots.

Election Night 2004 was no different from other election nights in this pattern of different network projections. Sometimes the gaps in timing were as large as several hours, sometimes all were made within minutes of each other. Typically when projections are made very close to each other, that means that Edison/Mitofsky (or VNS and VRS in earlier years) made the projection and the networks followed suit. (The exception to this rule, of course, is the Bush call in Florida on Election Night 2000, when it was Fox that triggered the other networks to make the same projections.) When there are major gaps between the times of the network projections, competition is clearly in operation. Unfortunately, competition almost invariably comes at the expense of accuracy. As long as networks compete in making projections, the chance of another miscall, and perhaps another situation like Election Night 2000, remains substantial.

The only time when the networks did not compete in making calls was in 1990 and 1992, when all the networks relied solely on the decisions made by VRS (Voter Research Service, the predecessor to VNS and Edison/Mitofsky), and there were no erroneous calls. CNN Political Director Tom Hannon referred to that time period as the "halcyon days," when responsibility for making the projections was on the consortium and there was no pressure on each network to call the races quickly. "I'd love to go back to 1990 and 1992 if the genie could be put back into the bottle," Hannon said in a post-election interview. "I take no pleasure from sweating in a control booth and making egregiously incorrect calls."[28]

IF THE NETWORKS are serious about eliminating competition in making projections, they should consider changing their National Election Poll (NEP) contract so that each network would agree not to make any projection of winners in any state until Edison/Mitofsky has first recommended it. The penalty for violating that part of the agreement could be a hefty fine, perhaps a million dollars. Or there could be no fine, with just the dishonor of breaking a public promise as the main deterrent from violating the contract. No network would be allowed to be part of the NEP without agreeing to that provision. The restriction would not prevent a network from waiting longer than Edison/Mitofsky to make a call, if the network's decision team felt Edison/Mitofsky had projected a winner too soon. But the restriction would prevent any single network from jumping the gun, and perhaps inducing other networks to follow.

It's no doubt too late to incorporate this provision in time for the 2006 and 2008 elections, but after that the networks should at least consider it. If there are any miscalls by the networks in 2006 or 2008, but none by Edison/Mitofsky, the case for this provision would be even stronger. This approach implicitly rejects the CBS philosophy that sees as much harm in calling a race late as in calling it too early. As William Adams points out, CBS already has a good solution for how to characterize races that have not yet been called. Instead of saying the race it "too close to call," the network posts the words "insufficient data" by the names of states where no projections have been made.[29] While

the other networks have not adopted this approach, they could probably be persuaded to do so.

Given the Democratic bias in many of the exit polls, that still
means that many Democratic states could be called before Republican
states, even though victory margins might be similar. But some states
also show a Republican bias in the exit polls, and in the long run there
is never any assurance that the pattern will remain as it is. It could be
in the future that typically Republicans would be more likely to participate in the polls, thus making the exit polls biased in that direction.
In any case, the goal of avoiding miscalls should transcend any short-
term problem with the timing of projections. With renewed caution
and education about what delayed calls mean, the fact of a delayed call
by itself should have no impact on voter turnout. The net benefit is that
a repeat of the fiasco of election 2000 would be far less likely, if not
completely preventable.

CBS News President Andrew Heyward acknowledged at the Congressional hearings, the miscalls made by the networks on Election
Night 2000 were not only "deeply embarrassing," but were "damaging
to our most important asset—our hard-won credibility."[30] Yet, despite
the apparent caution on Election Night 2004, the networks have not
fully addressed the fundamental problem that led to the most egregious
error on Election Night 2000—network competition. Instead, they
have blamed VNS for technical matters and hired a new operation that
is updated technically, but little changed from VNS or VRS in the models or the basic way data are collected and analyzed. In January 2004,
Mitofsky made this very point when he described to the *Chicago Tribune*
the new system he and his colleague, Joe Lenski, were directing.
"These are the same models [as those in the VNS system]. I would say
the changes are subtle. . . . They've all agreed to use the same criteria."[31]
That didn't sit well with Linda Mason, the vice president of public

affairs at CBS News, and an NEP representative. She acknowledged that "the overall big plan, the schematics, remain the same . . . but the utilization is different, the methods of collection are different, and technology has improved so much. So it's not the same." Instead, "It's been changed dramatically," she said. "What he [Mitofsky] said was not what he meant to say, I understand." But Mitofsky did mean what he said, though NEP put him under a gag order so he could not further embarrass the networks.[32]

This effort to spin Edison/Mitofsky as a new and improved system is not a good sign. By blaming VNS for the problems and dressing up the new Edison/Mitofsky election night projection system as though it is a radical departure from the previous VNS system, the network executives give the impression that they have corrected the problems that led to the miscalls on Election Night 2000. All they've really done is gloss over the fundamental cause of the problems, network competition, which they say is bad but don't want to address.

And then there's the Fox factor—getting information from politicians who have an axe to grind. Fox's approval of phone conversations between John Ellis and the Bush brothers on Election Night 2000 suggests that such contacts can still occur. The new de facto Fox decision team leader is John Gorman, who Ellis claimed was in frequent contact with members of the Democratic Party on Election Night 2000. Whether Gorman or his colleague, Arnon Mishkin, continue either to share consortium data with the Democrats or to solicit information from the Democrats, as Ellis claimed they did, is unknown. Nor is it known if there are Republicans on the team who engage in similar contacts with GOP representatives.[33] But the fact that the Fox network chief, Roger Ailes, lauds such contacts is not reassuring. The calls should be made on the basis of what the data show, not on what politicians would like the networks to do.

When asked if the errors of Election Night 2000 could ever happen again, NBC Director of Elections Sheldon Gawiser responded immediately, "Absolutely!" There's always some chance of making errors when projecting winners, though the chances of doing so now, he thinks, are smaller than they were in 2000. One reason for the lower likelihood, he said, is that the "balance has shifted toward being more careful than being quicker."[34] But as we saw in 1980, when NBC first used exit polls to project the races and beat the competition, and again in 1994, when ABC abandoned its reliance on VNS so the network could "kill them fuckers!," the balance can quickly shift in the other direction.

"They were careful in 2004," Edelman said of the network decision teams. "The 2000 election was still fresh. But they will start edging back . . . they have a culture of competition." How long before they repeat the errors of Election 2000? Edelman's response: "It's just a matter of time."[35]

Notes

PREFACE

1 See Andrew Gumbel, *Steal This Vote: Dirty Elections and the Rotten History of Democracy in America* (New York: Nation Books, 2005) for a detailed account of how votes and elections have been stolen.

CHAPTER 1 Irreparable Harm—An Overview

1 Jane Mayer, "Dept. of Close Calls," *The New Yorker*, Nov. 20, 2000, p. 38.
2 John Ellis, "A Hard Day's Night: John Ellis' Firsthand Account of Election Night," *Inside*, Dec. 11 and Dec. 26, 2000.
3 All references to Cynthia Talkov's views are based on personal interviews with her, April 15 and April 28, 2005.
4 Jeffrey Toobin, *Too Close to Call: The Thirty-Six-Day Battle to Decide the 2000 Election* (New York: Random House, 2001), p. 20.
5 The study was sponsored by *The Washington Post*, *The Chicago Tribune*, *The New York Times*, *The Wall Street Journal*, *The Palm Beach Post*, *The St. Petersburg Times*, and the Associated Press.
6 "Chads, Scanners, and Votes," CBS News Web site, Nov. 12, 2001. (http://www.cbsnews.com/stories/2001/11/12/politics/main317662.shtml). See also Robert Tanner and Sharon L. Crenson, "Florida Review Shows Narrowest Margin," AP news release, *Portsmouth Herald*, Nov. 12, 2001 (http://www.seacoastonline.com/2001news/11_12_w2.htm).

7 John F. Harris, "A Symbolic but Muddled Victory," *The Washington Post*, Nov. 12, 2001, p. A11 (http://www.washingtonpost.com/ac2/wp-dyn/A12604-2001Nov11?language=printer.)

8 Toobin, *Too Close to Call.*, p. 25.

9 Reed Irvine and Cliff Kincaid, "Lasting Damage from Election Night Numbers," Media Monitor on www.aim.org, Nov. 24, 2000.

10 Hannity quoted in Daphne Eviatar, "Murdoch's Fox News," *The Nation*, March 12, 2001.

11 Irvine and Kincaid, *Lasting Damage.*

12 David A. Kaplan, *The Accidental President* (New York: William Morrow, 2001), p. 28.

13 Toobin, *To Close to Call*, pp. 35, 56–57.

14 Todd Gitlin, "How TV Killed Democracy on Nov. 7," *Los Angeles Times*, Feb. 14, 2001.

15 Mickey Kaus, "Everything the New York Times Thinks About the Florida Recount Is Wrong!" *Slate*, posted Tuesday, Nov. 13, 2001.

16 Representative Peter Deutsch, in remarks at the hearing before the House Committee on Energy and Commerce, Feb. 14, 2001.

17 Cited in Vincent Bugliosi, *The Betrayal of America: How the Supreme Court Undermined the Constitution and Chose Our President* (New York: Thunder's Mouth Press/Nation Books, 2001), p. 51.

18 Kaplan, *Accidental President*, pp. 284–285.

19 Warren Mitofsky, written comments to a colleague, shortly after the November 2000 election.

20 Seth Mnookin, "It Happened One Night," *Brill's Content*, Feb. 4, 2001.

21 Jack Shafer, "Defending the Projectionists," *Slate*, posted Nov. 15, 2000, at 2:24 P.M. PT.

22 Quoted in Joe Hagan, "As Mercury Croons, Dan Rather Offers," *The New York Observer*, March 3, 2004.

CHAPTER 2 Election Night Projections—A Brief History

1 This discussion on the history of media competition comes from David W. Moore, *The Super Pollsters: How They Measure and Manipulate Public Opinion in America* (New York: Four Walls Eight Windows, 1995), pp. 249–299. See also Warren Mitofsky and Murray Edelman, "Election Night Estimation," Morris H. Hansen Lecture, Washington Statistical Society, Nov. 13, 2001.

2 Mitofsky and Lenski, p. 4; Moore, *Super Pollsters*, pp. 253.

3 Moore, *Super Pollsters*, pp. 254–257.

4 Ibid., pp.264–266; Mitofsky and Edelman, "Election Night Estimating," 9–10.

5 The material about John Blydenburgh is based on a personal interview with him, Jan. 6, 2006.

6 Moore, *Super Pollsters*, p. 266.

7 References to Murray Edelman's views are based on a personal interview with him, Jan. 4, 2006.

8 Rich Morin, "Networks to Dissolve Exit Poll Service: Replacement Sought for Election surveys," *The Washington Post*, Jan. 4, 2003, p. A03.

9 Rich Morin, "Bad Call in Florida," *The Washington Post*, Nov. 13, 2000, p. A27.

10 Warren Mitofsky, phone interview with author, March 22, 2006.

11 Murray Edelman, interview, Jan. 4, 2006.

12 Tribute from the three journalists who reviewed Election Night 2000 for CNN, in Joan Konner, James Risser, and Ben Wattenberg, *Television's Performance on Election Night 2000: A Report for CNN*, January 29, 2001, p. 24.

CHAPTER 3 "Hell to Pay"

1 The description of what happened on Election Night 2000 with the CBS/CNN joint decision team is based on personal observation.

2 David W. Moore, *The Super Pollsters: How They Measure and Manipulate Public Opinion in America* (New York: Four Walls Eight Windows, 1995).

3 Linda Mason, Kathleen Frankovic, and Kathleen Hall Jamieson, *CBS News Coverage of Election Night 2000: Investigation, Analysis, Recommendations*, report, CBS News, January, 2001, p. 26.

4 This estimate was presented by Warren Mitofsky and Murray Edelman, "Election Night Estimation," Morris H. Hansen Lecture, Washington Statistical Society, Nov. 13, 2001, p. 14.

CHAPTER 4 The "Cool" Cousins

1 All references to what happened on Election Night 2000 with the Fox decision team and to Cynthia Talkov's views are based on personal interviews with Cynthia Talkov on April 15 and April 28, 2005.

2 Ellis quoted in Jake Tapper, *Down and Dirty: The Plot to Steal the Presidency* (Boston: Little, Brown), p. 24.

3 Roger Ailes, prepared statement, in *Election Night Coverage by the Networks*, Hearing before the Committee on Energy and Commerce, U.S. House of Representatives (serial number 107–25), Feb. 14, 2001, pp. 116–118.

4 John Ellis, "A Hard Day's Night: John Ellis' Firsthand Account of Election Night," *Inside*, Dec. 11, 2000, p 1.

5 Ibid.

6 Ibid.

7 Murray Edelman, author interview, Jan. 4, 2006.

8 Ellis, "Hard Day's Night," p. 4.

9 Ibid.

10 All the networks retrieved their calling times, and VNS did so as well. The results were published in, among other places, Linda Mason, Kathleen Frankovic, and Kathleen Hall Jamieson, *CBS News Coverage of Election Night 2000: Investigation, Analysis, Recommendations*, report, CBS News, January

2001, p. 12. In the CBS report, however, the retraction times are included only for CBS/CNN and VNS. However, I personally kept a record of those retraction times, recorded on Election Night 2000.

11 Ellis, "Hard Day's NIght," p. 5.

12 Talkov, April 15, 2005, inverview.

13 Talkov, March 2, 2004, interview. This was the first time I heard that Ellis' call was prompted not by the data, but by Jeb Bush's exhortation to Ellis that the call be made. However, Talkov had shared that information with Mitofsky and Lenski at about four in the morning after Election Day 2000, when she called to tell them: "You won't believe what happened."

14 Talkov, April 15, 2005, interview.

15 Ellis, "Hard Day's Night, p. 5.

CHAPTER 5 The Bandwagon

1 Jack Shafer, "Defending the Projectionists," *Slate*, posted Nov. 15, 2000, at 2:24 P.M. PT.

2 Murray Edelman, author interview, Jan. 4, 2006.

3 Ibid. Lenski and Mitofsky confirm the memo in Joe Lenski and Warren Mitofsky, "Florida Timeline Election Night 2000," report, Nov. 27, 2000, p. 10.

4 The spreadsheets and the Edelman memo were sent to me on March 13, 2006, by David Pace of the Associated Press, who was the AP decision team leader on Election Night 2000.

5 Lenski and Mitofsky, "Florida Timeline Election Night 2000," pp. 6–7.

6 John Ellis, "A Hard Day's Night: John Ellis' Firsthand Account of Election Night," *Inside* magazine, Dec. 11, 2000.

7 Jeff Leeds, "Bush's Cousin Monitored Vote for Fox News," *Los Angeles Times*, Nov. 14, 2000.

8 Ellis, "Hard Day's Night."

9 Warren Mitofsky, communication to a colleague, shortly after the publication of Ellis' article on Dec. 11, 2000, sent to me on Apr. 25, 2005.

10 Prepared statement of Roger Ailes, chairman and CEO, Fox News Network, Hearing before the Committee on Energy and Commerce, U.S. House of Representatives, Feb. 14, 2001 serial no. 107–25, pp. 116–118. "I am aware that Mr. Ellis was speaking to then Governor George W. Bush and Jeb Bush on election night. Obviously, through his family connections, Mr. Ellis has very good sources. I do not see this as a fault or shortcoming of Mr. Ellis. Quite the contrary, I see this as a good journalist talking to his very high level sources on election night."

11 Ellis, "Hard Day's Night."

12 *Election Night Coverage by the Networks*, p. 124. Committee Chairman Billy Tauzin posed the question to the VNS executive director, Ted Savaglio: "The screen also says that for Al Gore to have a chance to carry Florida at that moment on that screen he needed to get 63 percent of the vote." Savaglio: "Right."

13 *Ellis.*

14 Mitofsky, communication to a colleague.

15 Sheldon Gawiser, author interview, Feb. 9, 2006.

16 Ibid.

17 Clyde Tucker, author interview, May 13, 2005.

18 Trevor Tompson, author interview, March 15, 2006.

19 Lenski and Mitofsky, "Florida Timeline Election Night 2000," p. 7.

20 Linda Mason, Kathleen Frankovic, and Kathleen Hall Jamieson, *CBS News Coverage of Election Night 2000: Investigation, Analysis, Recommendations*, report, CBS News, Jan., 2001, p. 21.

21 Gawiser, interview.

22 Lenski and Mitofsky, "Florida Timeline Election Night 2000."

23 Mason, Frankovic, and Jamieson, *CBS News Coverage of Election Night 2000*, p. 10.

24 Warren Mitofsky, letter to author, April 26, 2006.

25 Ibid.

26 Lenski and Mitofsky, "Florida Timeline Election Night 2000," p. 8.

27 See chapter 1 , p. 5, and chapter 1, note 4.

28 David Pace, author interview, March 13, 2006. See also pp. 84–86 on Pace's reaction to the networks' projections.

29 Lenski and Mitofsky, "Florida Timeline Election Night 2000," p. 8.

30 Alicia Shepherd, "How They Blew It," *American Journalism Review,* January–February, 2001.

31 John Blydenburgh, author interview, Jan. 6, 2006.

32 Alicia Shepherd, "How They Blew It."

33 References to Pace's views are based on Pace, author interview.

34 Shepherd, "How They Blew It."

35 Ibid.

CHAPTER 6 Scapegoat

1 Eric Schmitt, "Counting the Vote: House Republicans, GOP Lawmakers, See Bias by Networks in Calling Races," *New York Times*, Nov. 17, 2000.

2 "Did Networks Discourage Voters?" CBS News, Nov. 16, 2000.

3 Ibid.

4 *Election Night Coverage by the Networks*, Hearing before the Committee on Energy and Commerce, U.S. House of Representatives (serial number 107–25), Feb. 14, 2001, pp. 8–9.

5 In the CBS after-election report, Kathleen Frankovic reviews the many claims of depressed voter turnout over the years, including the 10,000-vote figure mentioned by AIM; see Kathleen Frankovic, "Analysis of Research: Do Early Calls Affect Voter Turnout?" in Linda Mason, Kathleen Frankovic, and Kathleen Hall Jamieson, *CBS News Coverage of Election Night 2000: Investigation, Analysis, Recommendations*, report, CBS News, January 2001, pp. 70–79.

6 Ibid., p. 3.

7 Kathryn Q. Seelye, "Network Chiefs Get Flogging at Capitol for Election Fiasco," *New York Times*, Feb. 15, 2001.

8 *Election Night Coverage by the Networks*, p. 31.

9 Ibid., p. 3.

10 Ibid., p. 116.

11 Ibid., p. 90.

12 Ibid., p. 96.

13 Alicia Shepherd, "How They Blew It," *American Journalism Review*, January–February, 2001.

14 *Election Night Coverage by the Networks*, p. 177: letter from David Westin, President of ABC News, to Rep. John D. Dingell, April 9, 2001.

15 Ibid., p. 117, prepared statement of Roger Ailes.

16 Cynthia Talkov and Inga Parsons, author interviews, April 26, 2006.

17 *Election Night Coverage by the Networks*, p. 117: prepared statement of Roger Ailes.

18 John Ellis, "A Hard Day's Night: John Ellis' Firsthand Account of Election Night," *Inside*, Dec. 11, 2000, pp. 3–4.

19 Jane Mayer, "Dept. of Close Calls: George W. Bush's Cousin," *The New Yorker*, Nov. 20, 2000, p. 38.

20 "Flubs put spotlight on how networks call elections," Associated Press, Nov. 17, 2000, posted on the Web at 11:52 A.M. EST.

21 Ibid.

22 *Election Night Coverage by the Networks*, p. 8.

23 *Election Night Coverage by the Networks*, pp. 48–50: prepared statement of Paul Biemer.

24 Ibid., p. 48.

25 Ibid., p. 50.

26 Ibid., pp. 57–58: testimony of Paul Biemer in response to questions of Rep. Edward J. Markey.

CHAPTER 7 Theft of the Election

1 *Election Night Coverage by the Networks*, Hearing before the Committee on Energy and Commerce, U.S. House of Representatives (serial number 107–25), Feb. 14, 2001, pp. 172–173.

2 John Ellis, "A Hard Day's Night: John Ellis' Firsthand Account of Election Night," *Inside*, Dec. 11, 2000.

3 Greg Palast, *The Best Democracy Money Can Buy: An Investigative Reporter Exposes the Truth About Globalization, Corporate Cons, and High-Finance Fraudsters* (New York: Plume, expanded election edition, May 2004).

4 Ibid., p. 57.

5 Melanie Eversley, "Firm Says Florida Was Warned About Voters Being Denied," *Palm Beach Post—Cox News Service,* April 1, 2001.

6 Palast, *Best Democracy,* p. 59.

7 Lee's testimony about DBT's actions and the unwillingness of Florida officials to make changes that would make the purge list more accurate were reported by both Palast, *Best Democracy,* p. 59, and by Eversley, "Firms Say Florida."

8 Lance deHaven-Smith, *The Battle for Florida* (Gainesville: University Press of Florida, 2005), p. 265.

9 Palast, *Best Democracy,* p. 50 (photocopy).

10 Katherine Harris, "A Florida Makeover," *Harper's,* July 2002, reprinted on http://www.gregpalast.com/detail.cfm?artid=167&row=2.

11 Greg Palast, "Katherine Harris Says Palast 'Twisted and Maniacal'—in July's Harper's," *Harper's,* July 2002.

12 Palast, *Best Democracy,* p. 70.

13 Ibid., p. 36.

14 Ibid., p. 34.

15 Ibid., p. 71

16 Lance deHaven-Smith, *Battle for Florida,* p. 209.

17 Ibid.

18 Ibid., p. 210.

19 Ibid.

20 Ibid., p. 252.

21 Ibid., p. 251.

22 Ibid., p. 252.

23 Ibid., p. xii.

24 Palast, *Best Democracy,* p. 80.

25 DeHaven-Smith, *Battle for Florida,* p. xii.

26 Ibid., p. xiii.

27 Ibid.

28 Ibid.

29 Alan M. Dershowitz, *Supreme Injustice: How the High Court Hijacked Election 2000* (New York: Oxford University Press, 2001).

30 Vincent Bugliosi, *The Betrayal of America: How the Supreme Court Undermined the Constitution and Chose the Next President* (New York: Thunder's Mouth Press/Nation Books, 2001).

31 Dershowitz, *Supreme Injustice,* p. 5.

32 Cited in Margaret Jane Radin, "Can the Rule of Law Survive *Bush v. Gore?*" in Bruce Ackerman, ed., *Bush v. Gore: The Question of Legitimacy* (New Haven: Yale University Press, 2002), p. 115.

33 Jed Rubenfeld, "Not as Bad as *Plessy.* Worse," in Ackerman, *Bush v. Gore,* p. 22 (emphasis added).

34 David Kairys, "*Bush v. Gore* Blues," *Jurist,* May 19, 2001; available at http://jurist.law.pitt.edu/forum/forumnew23.htm.

35 Rubenfeld, "Not as Bad as *Plessy.* Worse," p. 22.

36 Ibid., p. 24.

37 Ibid., p. 26.

38 Cited in Bugliosi, *Betrayal of America*, p. 57.

39 Cited in ibid., pp. 96–97.

40 Ibid., p. 44.

41 Ibid.

42 "Newspaper: Butterfly Ballot Cost Gore White House," CNN, reporting on *Palm Beach Post* study, March 11, 2001.

43 Jonathan N. Wand, Kenneth W. Shotts, Jasjeet S. Sekhon, Walter R. Mebane, Jr., Michael C. Herron, and Henry E. Brady, "The Butterfly Did It: The Aberrant Vote for Buchanan in Palm Beach County, Florida," *American Political Science Review,* vol. 95, no. 4 (December 2001) pp. 793–810.

44 See Jeffrey Toobin, *Too Close to Call: The Thirty-Six-Day Battle to Decide the 2000 Eleciton* (New York: Random House, 2001), 172–173.

45 Rubenfeld, "Not as Bad as *Plessy.* Worse," p. 26.

46 Ibid., p. 27.

47 Dershowitz, *Supreme Injustice*, p. 81.

48 "Can the Rule of Law Survive *Bush v. Gore?*" p.117; Radin is a professor at Stanford Law School.

49 Kairys, "*Bush v. Gore* Blues."

50 Dershowitz, *Supreme Injustice*, p. 123 (citing *U.S. v. Virginia*, 5118 U.S. 515, 596 (1996), Scalia dissenting).

51 Ibid., p. 132.

52 Ibid., p. 4.

53 Most of the information in the next few pages about what happened with the appeals comes from Jeffrey Toobin, *Too Close to Call: The Thirty-Six-Day Battle to Decide the 2000 Election* (New York: Random House, 2001).

54 Cited in Ibid., p. 236.

55 Ibid., p. 245.

56 Ibid., p. 250.

57 Ibid. Also cited in Bugliosi, *Betrayal of America*, p. 52.

58 Toobin, *Too Close to Call*, p. 250 (emphasis added).

59 Dershowitz, *Supreme Injustice*, p. 127.

60 Bugliosi, *Betrayal of America*, p. 48.

61 Lawrence Tribe, *eroG .v hsuB*: Through the Looking Glass," in Bruce Ackerman, *Bush v. Gore: The Question of Legitimacy* (New Haven: Yale University Press, 2002), p. 42.

62 Dershowitz, *Supreme Injustice*, p. 62.

63 See Dershowitz, *Supreme Injustice*, pp. 121–172 for his analysis of the motives of the justices.

64 David A. Kaplan, *The Accidental President* (New York: William Morrow, 2001), pp. 284–285.

65 Throughout *Supreme Injustice*, Dershowitz refers to the "corruption" of the U.S. Supreme Court justices, and their "unprincipled" behavior. See, for example pp. 178, 197.

66 Bugliosi, *Betrayal of America*, p. 48.

67 Cited in Toobin, *To Close to Call*, p. 280.

CHAPTER 8 Election 2004—Another Uproar

1 When I greeted Mitofsky on Election Night 2004, it was in my new role (new in 2004) as CNN's contact person at Edison/Mitofsky headquarters. The CNN decision team was located in Atlanta; if they had a question about the data coming from Edison/Mitofsky, they could call me at a dedicated line so that I could personally track down the right person and get the information. To avoid any conflict of interest with my employer, the Gallup Organization, I performed this service without compensation.

2 Rich Morin, "Networks to Dissolve Exit Poll Service," *The Washington Post*, Jan. 14, 2003, p. A03.

3 Murray Edelman, author interview, Jan. 4, 2006.

4 Ibid.

5 Rich Morin and Claudia Deane, "Exit Polls in Doubt for Nov. Election," *The Washington Post*, Aug. 16, 2002.

6 Ibid.

7 Alessandra Stanley, "The 2002 Elections: The Pollster Man at the Uneasy Helm of Voter Survey Service," *New York Times*, Nov. 7, 2002.

8 Morin, "Networks to Dissolve Exit Poll Service."

9 Ibid.

10 Matthew David, "Bin Laden Threats May Boost Bush," BBC News (http://news.bbc.co.uk/2/hi/middle_east/4630054.stm). No date of posting, but clearly before the election results of Nov. 2, 2004, were known.

11 Howard Kurtz, "TV News Plays It Safe, Up to a Point," *The Washington Post*, Nov. 3, 2004, p. A23.

12 Mike Curtin, author interview, Feb. 9, 2006.

13 For the problems encountered by voters in Ohio, see Mark Crispin Miller, "None Dare Call It Stolen: Ohio, the Election, and America's Servile Press," *Harper's*, September, 2005.

14 Howard Kurtz, "They Don't Declare: The Vote Callers Who Lost Their Voice," *The Washington Post*, Nov. 4, 2004, p. C01, reporting a statement by NBC News Vice President Bill Wheatley.

15 Warren Mitofsky, speaking on the morning of Nov. 3, 2004, and essentially repeated in interview on Feb. 2, 2006.

16 Phil Rosenthal, "For Hours We Knew What They Wouldn't Say," *Chicago Sun-Times*, Nov. 4, 2004.

17 Fox Senior News Vice President John Moody said no call was made for Nevada because of reservations about the state's data, as cited in Kurtz, "They Don't Declare." In a personal interview on Feb. 9, 2006, Sheldon Gawiser told me that it was "absolutely incorrect" that the NBC decision team that he heads failed to call Nevada for fear of giving Bush 270 electoral votes.

18 Kurtz, "TV News Plays It Safe."

19 Kurtz, "They Don't Declare."

20 Jim Rutenberg, "Report Says Problems Led to Skewed Surveying Data," *New York Times*, Nov. 5, 2006.

21 Jacques Steinberg, "Report: Human Factors Skewed Exit Poll Results," *New York Times* News Service, Jan. 20, 2005.

22 Ibid.

23 Joe Lenski, author interview, Feb. 9, 2006.

24 Julia Malone, "As inquiry into Faulty Exit Polls Unfolds, Conspiracy Theories Grow," *Palm Beach Post-Cox News Service*, Nov. 23, 2004.

25 Steven F. Freeman, "The Unexplained Exit Poll Discrepancy: Part I," University of Pennsylvania, Center for Organized Dynamics, working paper #04-10, Nov. 22, 2004, p. 2.

26 Jonathan D. Simon and Ron P. Baiman, "The 2004 Presidential Election: Who Won The Popular Vote? An Examination of the Comparative Validity of Exit Poll and Vote Count Data," report, *Free Press*, Jan. 2, 2005 http://freepress.org/images/departments/PopularVotePaper181_1.pdf.

27 Edison Media Research and Mitofsky International, *Evaluation of Edison/Mitofsky Election System 2004*, report, p. 31.

28 Ibid., p. 4.

29 USCountVotes "Response to Edison/Mitofsky Election System 2004 Report," Jan. 31, 2005.

    Contributors and supporters include:

    Josh Mitteldorf, Ph.D.—Temple University Statistics Department

    Kathy Dopp, M.S. in mathematics—USCountVotes, president

    Steven F. Freeman, Ph.D.—Visiting scholar and affiliated faculty, Center for Organizational Dynamics, University of Pennsylvania

    Brian Joiner, Ph.D.—professor of statistics and director of statistical consulting (ret.), University of Wisconsin

    Frank Stenger, Ph.D.—Professor of numerical analysis, School of Computing, University of Utah

    Richard G. Sheehan, Ph.D.—Professor, Department of Finance, University of Notre Dame

    Elizabeth Liddle, M.A.—(UK) Ph.D. candidate at the University of Nottingham

    Paul F. Velleman, Ph.D.—Associate professor, Department of Statistical Sciences, Cornell University

    Victoria Lovegren, Ph.D.—Lecturer, Department of Mathematics, Case Western Reserve University

Campbell B. Read, Ph.D.—Professor emeritus, Department of Statistical Science, Southern Methodist University

Also peer-reviewed by USCountVotes' core group of statisticians and independent reviewers.

30 "Analysis of the 2004 Presidential Election Exit Poll Discrepancies: Response to the Edison/Mitofsky Election System 2004 Report," USCountVotes' National Election Data Archive Project, March 31, 2005, updated April 12, 2005. Authors and endorsers include:

Ron Baiman, Ph.D.—Institute of Government and Public Affairs, University of Illinois at Chicago

Kathy Dopp, M.S. in mathematics, —USCountVotes, president

Steven F. Freeman, Ph.D.—Visiting scholar and affiliated faculty, Center for Organizational Dynamics, University of Pennsylvania

Brian Joiner, Ph.D.—Professor of statistics and director of statistical consulting (ret.), University of Wisconsin

Victoria Lovegren, Ph.D.—Lecturer, Department of Mathematics, Case Western Reserve University

Josh Mitteldorf, Ph.D.—Temple University Statistics Department

Campbell B. Read, Ph.D.—Professor emeritus, Department of Statistical Science, Southern Methodist University

Richard G. Sheehan, Ph.D.—Professor, Department of Finance, University of Notre Dame

Jonathan Simon, J.D.—Alliance for Democracy

Frank Stenger, Ph.D.—Professor of numerical analysis, School of Computing, University of Utah

Paul F. Velleman, Ph.D.—Associate professor, Department of Statistical Sciences, Cornell University

Bruce O'Dell—USCountVotes, vice president

This report has been reviewed via USCountVotes' email discussion list for statisticians, mathematicians, and pollsters.

31 Mark Blumenthal as the Mystery Pollster, "The Liddle Model That Could," April 29, 2005 (http://www.mysterypollster.com/main/2005/04/the_liddle_mode.html).

32 Bruce O'Dell, "Response to US Count Votes' Working Paper 'Patterns of Exit Poll Discrepancies: On the Implausibility of a "Uniform" Bias Explanation of the 2004 Presidential Election Exit Poll Discrepancies' May 12, 2005," (http://www.digitalagility.com/data/ODell_Response_to_USCV_Working_Paper.pdf), June 1, 2005.

33 Dick Morris, "Those Faulty Exit Polls Were Sabotage," The Hill, Nov. 4, 2004.

34 John Wambaugh, "Election 2004: Exit-Poll Disinformation Hoax Backfires?" Renew America,. Jan. 7, 2005 (http://www.renewamerica.us/columns/wambough/050107).

35 Rich Morin, "Surveying the Damage: Exit Polls Can't Predict Winners, So Don't Expect Them To," *The Washington Post*, Nov. 21, 2004, p. B01.

36 Keith Olbermann, "Zogby vs. Mitofsky," Keith Olbermann's Blog (http://www.yuricareport.com/ElectionAftermath04/OlbermannZogbyVs-Mitofsky.html), Nov. 24, 2004, 9:18 A.M. ET.

37 Nick Anderson and Faye Fiore, "Early Data for Kerry Proved Misleading," *Los Angeles Times*, Nov. 4, 2004.

38 Jack A. Shafer, "The Official Excuses for the Bad Exit Poll Numbers Don't Cut It," *Slate*, Nov. 6, 2004, at 12:23 A.M. ET.

39 Nick Panagakis, posted on a Web site of the American Association for Public Opinion Research, AAPORNET, Nov. 6, 2004.

40 Morin, "Surveying the Damage.,"

41 William Douglas, "Exit Polls Come Under Fire," Knight-Ridder Newspapers, Nov. 3, 2004.

CHAPTER 9 Never Say Never Again

1 Joan Konner, James Risser, and Ben Wattenberg, *Television's Performance on Election Night 2000: A Report for CNN*, Jan. 29, 2001, p. 6, emphasis added.

2 Warren Mitofsky, author interview, March 13, 2006.

3 Warren Mitofsky, "The Future of Exit Polling," Public Opinion Pros, Jan. 2006 (http://www.publicopinionpros.com/op_ed/2006/jan/mitofsky.asp).

4 Method Statement, National Election Pool Exit Polls, Nov. 2, 2004.

5 Linda Mason, Kathleen Frankovic, and Kathleen Hall Jamieson, *CBS News Coverage of Election Night 2000: Investigation, Analysis, Recommendations*, report CBS News, Jan. 2001, p. 26.

6 William C. Adams, *Election Night News and Voter Turnout: Solving the Projection Puzzle* (Boulder, CO: Lynne Rienner Publishers, Inc., 2005, pp. 1, 127.

7 Kathleen Frankovic, "Analysis of Research: Do Early Calls Affect Voter Turnout?" in Mason, Frankovic, and Jamieson, *CBS News Coverage of Election Night 2000*, p. 70.

8 Adams, *Election Night News and Voter Turnout: Solving the Projection Puzzle*, p. 129.

9 WTOP government guide (http://capwiz.com/wtop/issues/bills/?bill=35256&size=full), Jan. 22, 2001.

10 Adams, *Election Night News and Voter Turnout*, p. 10. See also UPI, "House Panel Backs Measure on Uniform Poll Closing Time," *The New York Times*, Oct. 11, 1985.

11 William Adams makes a "modest proposal" to deal with the early call problem. The proposal would need congressional approval but would not require a major change in voting times. The networks have already promised not to project winners in any state until all the polls have closed in that state. This reform means that the earliest a candidate could amass 270 electoral votes in states where the polls have closed would be 9:00 P.M. ET, two hours before the polls close on the

West Coast. That leaves two hours when a presidential winner theoretically could be announced, thus angering western voters who feel their vote is demeaned when they are essentially told it doesn't matter who they vote for because the winner has been decided. If the West Coast states extend Daylight Savings Time for two weeks in presidential election years, the earliest a presidential winner could be announced would be still be at 9:00 P.M. ET, but that would be 7:00 P.M. Pacific *Daylight* Time, or just one hour before the polls close in that time zone, cutting in half the amount of time when West Coast voters could be insulted by a network announcement of the presidential winner. Voters in Alaska and Hawaii could still be insulted for one and two more hours respectively. See Adams, *Election Night News and Voter Turnout*, pp. 133–134.

12 Konner, Risser, and Wattenberg, *Television's Performance on Election Night 2000*, p. 3.

13 Ibid.

14 Ibid., p. 5.

15 Ibid., p. 6.

16 Kathleen Frankovic, author interview, March 23, 2006.

17 Warren J. Mitofsky and Murray Edelman, "Election Night Estimation," Morris H. Hansen Lecture, Washington Statistical Society, Nov. 13, 2001, p. 10.

18 Warren Mitofsky and Joe Lenski, "Recommendations for Improving Criteria for Election Projections," January 25, 2001, included in appendix 5 in Konner, Risser, and Wattenberg, *Television's Performance on Election Night 2000*.

19 Ibid., p. ii.

20 Warren Mitofsky, author interview, March 22, 2006.

21 Ibid., p. i (emphasis added).

22 Ibid., p. iii.

23 Frankovic, author interview.

24 Warren Mitofsky, e-mail to author, March 15, 2006.

25 Frankovic, author interview.

26 Adams, *Election Night News and Voter Turnout*, p. 57, n. 19.

27 The projected times of calls are taken from an informal record made by CBS for its internal use, which Frankovic shared with me. All the CBS times are correct, taken from CBS's own record, but the other times have not been verified. I checked the CNN projection times on the CBS record with the CNN times listed on the CNN Web site, and in most cases only a couple of minutes separated the times. A few cases showed up to twenty minutes' difference, suggesting the CBS record is fairly accurate, but not exact.

28 Konner, Risser, and Wattenberg, *Television's Performance on Election Night 2000*, p. 27.

29 Adams, *Election Night News and Voter Turnout*, p. 57, n. 19.

30 *Election Night Coverage by the Networks, Hearing before the Committee on Energy and Commerce, U.S. House of Representatives* (serial no. 107-25), Feb. 14, 2001, p. 107: prepared statement of CBS News President Andrew Heyward.

31 Joe Hagan, "As Mercury Croons, Dan Rather Offers," *The New York Observer*, Mar. 5, 2004.

32 Ibid.

33 I requested an interview with John Gorman to discuss the activities of the Fox decision team, but he wrote to me on Mar. 22, 2006, "Under the terms of my contract with Fox they have final say on any interviews regarding work for them. They've decided that they would prefer I not give any interviews about the election nights. Sorry."

34 Sheldon Gawiser, author interview, Feb. 9, 2006.

35 Murray Edelman, author interview, March 14, 2006.

Index